The Black Sheep

By Web Maddox

Nortex Press

Copyright 1975 by Web Maddox

Published by Nortex Press

*Printed in the United States of America
All Rights Reserved*

ISBN 0-89015-079-6

PREFACE

The Western "Bad Man" has been the subject of so many short stories, magazine articles, moving pictures, and television plots, that the production of one more book may appear to be piling a small Pelion on a large Ossa— except that this one has a different concept of approach.

The Western "Bad Man" and his environmental frontier, where the good guy eventually triumphs over the bad guys, have been and remain the meat-and-potatoes of the motion picture industry, and today "Westerns" are being produced in Europe where ersatz cowboys and Indians are cheaper by the dozen. In the current elevation of sex as the almost exlcusive theme in literature and entertainment, only the Western can compete with the pornographic film for the customer's attention.

Gangsterism is a European importation, received along with undesirable immigrants such as the Mafia recruits or the flood of "wetbacks," but the Western "Bad Man"— white, native-born—is uniquely American in the annals of crime. He has disappeared with the frontier which beckoned irresistably to the young, footloose, and venturesome. And the ending of the frontier marked the end of the era of America's growth. That which ceases to grow begins to die of inner decay and corruption. With crime and violence rampant, and moral turpitude in high places, America may be approaching its twilight, unless a radical reassessment of values takes place. The bad man of the past was individualistic—bad men of today are a class.

We have gathered here some wool from five Black Sheep—three obstreperous rams and two wild and woolly ewes. Although excellence can be attained only by discrimination, we are forbidden by law to choose those whom we wish to employ, to work with or live with, and since this admonition also applies to gender, we have included two choice bits of femininity, assuming that a 3-2 ratio will be acceptable. In the vocation of outlaw, these

American women can take their place with the best—or worst.

This work is in no sense a reference or textbook. Most of the deeds of these characters have been detailed before—more or less accurately—and our effort here is to present the highlights, uncluttered with footnotes, references, and too many names, dates, and places. But there has been no sacrifice of authenticity. No words have been put into the mouths of our characters, and when conversations or statements are related, these have been vouchsafed by credible witnesses or capable reporters. Letters, official files, and other documents bear their own inherent validity. Our purpose is to tell you what these individuals looked like, how they lived and died, and what motivated them; to suggest the flavor of their times; and, finally, to learn how they appear in the eyes of a more sophisticated generation. There has been extensive and painstaking research which yielded some interesting incidents not known before. Personal knowledge of the areas in which our Black Sheep lived and operated has been helpful.

There is nothing funny about looking into the business end of a gun held in hands fully capable of pulling the trigger. In a very real sense, and not by way of pun, our Black Sheep were in dead earnest; nevertheless, knowing that they were infamously notorious, it appears that on occasion they carried out a particularly surprising or spectacular escapade just to enhance or live up to their reputations. And they frequently displayed a grim, sardonic wit and humor.

In short, we have attempted with words to bring our Black Sheep to life for you, so that from a safe distance in time and space, you may contemplate them for a few hours with, possibly, only a vicarious, slight trace of the anxiety with which their contemporaries would have encountered them.

As time has gone on, more and worse crimes than those perpetrated by our Black Sheep are committed daily in this turbulent world now and with little more than routine reporting and momentary shock. We grant that the so-called "good old days" were not always good, but a less permissive society found the exploits of our subjects at such appalling variance from the norm that their crimes were read of and discussed with frenetic fascination and a peculiarly lasting interest. An aura was created, and something of that psyche still persists about them. Hence the many books. Hence this book.

Web Maddox

DEDICATION

For Evelyn

ACKNOWLEDGEMENTS

Biographies of those long departed are seldom the work of one person, but rather a gleaning of information gathered from many sources. Accordingly, the sketches presented here relate only the highlights in criminal activities of the subjects and indicate the contemporary public interest in a world which had no rapid communication.

To those interested in knowing more about these men and women, the books listed in the bibliography are recommended. Most of them may be found in the reference rooms of public libraries. Some are remarkably well documented. Some are unfortunately out of print.

Many have contributed their help in various ways to this book. Among them are Evelyn Oppenheimer for patient and persistent encouragement, Marion Cutler for editing, the late James R. Record of the **Ft. Worth Star-Telegram** and Sheriff Lon Evans of Tarrant County. The author is grateful.

TABLE OF CONTENTS

PART I

    Clyde Barrow and Bonnie Parker 5

PART II

    John Wesley Hardin 49

PART III

    Sam Bass 85

PART IV

    Belle Starr 129

Bibliography 155

Appendix 157

Baa! Baa! black sheep

    have you any wool?

Yes, sir, yes, sir, three bags full:

One for my master, one for my dame

And one for the little boy

    that lives in the lane.

Mother Goose

BONNIE AND CLYDE overlooking a haul.

PART

1

Clyde Barrow

And Bonnie Parker

CLYDE BARROW with machine gun.

PROLOGUE

The great moving picture palace with its elaborate decor, luxuriously deep carpets, shaded lights, and carefully regulated temperature, was filled to capacity. A thrilling drama of high adventure, and hair-breadth escapes was being shown. It involved an extremely attractive and fascinating couple (played by handsome, youthful Henry Fonda, and glamourous Sylvia Sidney); mutually dedicated lovers who had been forced into a life of crime and violence by a harsh, inequitable society; relentlessly pursued and hounded, like pitiful, desperate animals, by a cruel and malevolent police. The name of the movie was "You Only Live Once." The year was 1937.

The drama was based on the recently ended lives of a couple whose names had made newspaper headlines all over the country for two years. Spine-tingling, exciting action and superlative love, in the face of incredible danger, held the audience spell-bound. But, as with most things, moving pictures must come to an end, and, toward the end of this picture, doomed by inexorable fate, the devoted pair had taken refuge in a small cottage, which might have been on the outskirts of any large city. They were completely surrounded and besieged by a large force of police—enough men, weapons, equipment and ammunition to put down a Central American revolution. At the crescendo of violence, a bullet struck and mortally wounded the handsome hero. And as he lay dying, cradled in the arms of his weeping sweetheart, the racket of outside gunfire was stilled or muted long enough for the poignant, silvery voice of young Fonda to come floating through the theatre in a tremulous, heartbreaking farewell:

"Thank you . . . Thank you for loving me."

There were few dry eyes in the house.

It was not exactly like that with Clyde and Bonnie. In fact, it was not like that at all.

CLYDE AND BONNIE'S death car.

CLYDE BARROW
1909-1934

BONNIE PARKER
1910-1934

On the morning of May 23, 1934, the scene on the little gravelled road eighteen miles southeast of Arcadia, Louisiana, was one of rustic peace and simplicity. This is a region of piney woods and red soil; birds and insects were busy on their mid-morning foragings; the incense of pine and the perfume of Spring filled the air. Truly, one susceptible to the beauties of nature might have described it as idyllic, sylvan, bucolic, pastoral. But one more keenly attuned to the nuances of life and death would have felt intolerable suspense; and a sharp eye would have discovered six men secreted in a clump of bushes near an elevation in the road. They had lain or crouched there, quiet and alert, since the preceding night. Obviously, they were peace officers, and they had with them a machine gun, an automatic rifle, and four shotguns loaded with buckshot. The brush in which they were hidden was separated from the road by a bar pit, and their position on the slight eminence was a natural barricade. It was in the middle of a short, open stretch of road which sloped gently in each direction to pine forests.

At fifteen minutes after nine, a small truck emerged from the trees to the south, travelling north in the slow, measured manner common to such vehicles.

A few minutes later, a dusty gray sedan appeared from the north trees, and it was moving south. The automobile was being driven with more urgency, and trailing behind it was a cloud of red dust—ominous portent of what was soon to follow.

The driver of the car was a slender young man wearing a dark suit and blue shirt, and he was in stocking feet. Some years before, the large toe of his left foot had been severed, and it is said that an amputated member often aches in absentia. His eyes were shaded by dark glasses, and in his pockets was five hundred and seven dollars in currency. On one arm of the young man, the name "Gladys" was tattooed, and on the other was a similarly indelible "Anne." These were the names of previous loves.

His thin, blond, woman companion wore a red cotton dress, a white hat with red crown, silk stockings and red shoes. On her fingers were two inconspicuous diamond rings and a conventional gold wedding band. Other accessories included a small wrist watch and a brooch fashioned in the shape of three acorns. Invisible to the eye, a cross hung from a gold chain around her neck. On her right leg, a tattoo represented two intertwined hearts, one bearing the name "Roy."

There was nothing about the car to distinguish it from many similar vehicles; but the occupants had an unusually wary and guarded tautness. And the automobile carried a strange cargo. A machine gun lay across the lap of the young woman, and a pistol was within easy reach of the man. Other items of a small arsenal were two riot guns, three sub-machine guns, eight automatic pistols, a .38 caliber revolver, and two thousand rounds of ammunition in zippered bags. Sandwiched in between the guns were several sheets of music, and a saxophone. Blankets, assorted automobile license plates, miscellaneous clothing, a suitcase, a woman's overnight bag with the usual contents, a small amount of food, and two magazines—one of the romantic type, and the other a detective pulp—rounded out the list.

The truck was first to reach the summit of the road elevation and it started down the slope on the other side. The man in the gray sedan reduced his speed for the passing, and then the sedan in turn slowly topped the elevation. At this precise moment, one of the men in ambush yelled: "Halt!" And almost simultaneously, a fusillade of one hundred sixty-seven bullets from machine gun, rifle and shotguns riddled the car and its occupants. The woman uttered a dreadful scream—"Like a panther," one of the men said later. In just a few seconds, shattered glass and debris littered the road and the automobile, its engine dead, rolled gently some forty feet down the slope, and finally came to a stop against the dirt embankment of the bar pit. Presently, the men in the ambuscade stepped from concealment, and, guns drawn, approached the car with extreme caution. They might well have thrown caution to the morning breeze. Like the automobile engine, Clyde Barrow, Number One Public Enemy, and Bonnie Parker, his Gun Moll, were dead—quite dead. If the story of Clyde and Bonnie has any particular significance in the annals of American "unorganized" crimes of violence, it is for marking the end of an era of horse and six-shooter, and ushering in the new one of automobile and automatic.

Clyde Champion Barrow was born to illiterate farming parents in Ellis County, Texas (which adjoins Dallas County), on March 24, 1909. Relatives contended that his middle given name had really been Chestnut, and that the name Champion had been pinned on him by imaginative newspaper reporters. And in his particular area of activity, he deserved it.

There were eight children, including a brother, Buck, who managed to acquire a voluminous police record before his death, and a loyal sister whose name was Nellie. An Ellis County acquaintance recalled that "the Barrow boys were just about like any other young fellows." While Clyde was young, the family moved to what was then a mean and squalid section in the Trinity River Bottom of

West Dallas. Clyde had received only desultory schooling in Ellis County, and his school record in Dallas was principally a long list of truancies until he quit altogether, and went to work intermittently at various jobs. Soon after moving to the city, Clyde displayed a natural propensity for burglary and thievery, aided and abetted by the more experienced, older brother, Buck.

Since the Barrow boys had come from the country, it was natural that their early thefts involved familiar merchandise. They became poultry thieves. Under the tutelage of brother Buck, Clyde came to be considered an expert.

Among his arrests was one at Fort Worth on February 23, 1928, when Clyde, who was not quite nineteen, attended the wedding of a friend known as "King of the Chicken Thieves," who referred to Clyde as one of his boys. The following year Clyde was arrested again in Ft. Worth, this time for careless collision. The officers who booked him described Clyde as "just a dirty, greasy-looking punk, no different from a number of other sorry thieves."

Under the influence and pressures of the city, the Barrow brothers soon abandoned squawking chickens for more salable and sophisticated merchandise. Beginning with hubcaps, they progressed rapidly to tires and batteries and then the entire automobile. Clyde became proficient; even, we are told, "artistic" in filing and altering automobile engine numbers, changing paint and doing alterations which made identification difficult or impossible. A peace officer estimated that, during his short lifetime, Clyde Barrow stole at least three hundred automobiles. His favorite car for personal use was a Ford, because at that time it was the fastest of the stock cars, had the quickest take-off, and the added virtue of being varied in colors and models. He was later to document this preference in an unusual letter.

His first "violent" love affair was at the age of sixteen

with a girl named "Anne." Her parents were respectable people who objected very much to her association with Clyde, and sent her out of town to visit friends in the hope that she would forget her romantic inclinations. Clyde rented an automobile for the purpose of visiting her, but he did not return the car; instead he abandoned it and "borrowed" another, which more nearly suited his fancy. The net result was arrest and jail term. The affair with Anne terminated, but he had already had her name tattooed on his arm.

He recovered from this affair and returned one day from Wichita Falls, Texas, with a girl named "Gladys," whom he introduced and lived with as his wife, for a time. Her name was promptly tattoed on the other arm, leaving no other suitable place on his anatomy for similar exhibitions in the future. Although he and Gladys were never legally married, the arrangement constituted a common-law marriage in Texas. By this time, Clyde was an experienced and professional burglar and thief. But the proceeds realized were insufficient to support Gladys in the manner which she had expected, and she departed. After this, and until he met Bonnie, Clyde's principal companions were young men engaged in the same line of activity and the girls who usually associate with such characters.

Rowena is a small town in West Texas, between Ballinger and San Angelo. It was there that Bonnie Parker was born on October 1, 1910. She was, therefore, a year and a half younger than Clyde Barrow. She had an older brother, Hubert, who was called "Buster," and a younger sister named Billie.

Her father, a brick mason, died when Bonnie was about four years old. Mrs. Parker then moved to Dallas to live with her mother and got a job in order to support herself and her children. The home was in a section of town which was known as "Cement City," adjacent to the great cement plant in West Dallas. Bonnie attended the Cement

City School, and later, Bryan High School. But when she was sixteen, she married. Roy Thornton, the bridegroom, had a long criminal record, and Bonnie knew it. They lived for a while near Bonnie's mother, but Thornton's professional activities resulted in frequent absences, and the couple moved in with Mama.

They appeared to be compatible, but his unpredictable coming and going, his long absences and his failure to support Bonnie, and probably sheer boredom, led her to go to work.

She got a job as waitress at Marco's, a small, short-order cafe in downtown Dallas—a hangout near the court house for peace officers and the usual habitues of a court house district. The only necessary qualifications were ability to dish up short orders and to meet the public pleasantly. The latter ability Bonnie supposedly possessed to a marked degree. It was claimed that Bonnie, with her sparkling personality, was Marco's principal asset.

Judging from photographs of her, it cannot be said that she was beautiful or even pretty. She was small, little more than five feet tall, and very thin, weighing less than a hundred pounds. Her eyes were described as "very blue," and her hair, (said her mother) was a "mass of yellow curls." Her complexion was unusually good. Her mouth was extremely wide and thin, and her other features were sharp and hawk-like. (Unsympathetic peace officers have described her as "horse-faced and mannish-looking.") But she had youth, enormous energy and vitality, and her employment served to widen her acquaintanceship and horizons.

Roy Thornton's prolonged trips became unendurable. After one of his sudden reappearances in 1929, Bonnie decided she had had enough, and she showed him the door. The shattered romance left few, if any, scars. She may have looked ruefully from time to time at the name "Roy" tattooed on her leg, but she never went to the trouble of obtaining a divorce from him and when she died, she was legally the wife of Roy Thornton. Soon after she dismissed him from her home and life, he was required to leave Dallas on yet another journey: he was sentenced to a five year penitentiary term.

Bonnie's charms were not enough to keep the cash register ringing at Marco's. It closed down in the same year—1929—and Bonnie was out of a job.

There are two versions of how the Barrow and Parker meeting first came about. One has it that they were visiting mutual friends in a small Louisiana town. Another, and more likely version, is that Bonnie was at the home of a girl friend in Dallas when Clyde dropped in for a call. At any rate, when they did meet, they fell immediately in love. The fact that Bonnie had a legal husband in the penitentiary, and that Clyde was not divorced from a common-law wife, was of no consequence to the enamoured pair.

Clyde had already acquired a considerable criminal record. In 1926 he had been arrested for automobile theft and had served a short time in the penitentiary. Arrests for attempted thefts, burglary, and safe-cracking, were numerous.

He soon took up a casual sort of residence in the Parker home, and there, early one morning, he was taken into custody again. He was taken to Denton, Texas, where the charge of theft against him proved to be unsupported by sufficient evidence; but he was subsequently escorted to Waco, Texas, where he was also wanted. There, he confessed to a number of burglaries and thefts, five of automobiles.

Luckily, Clyde conveniently had a sister living in Waco, and there Bonnie proceeded, posthaste, grateful for an opportunity to prove her loyalty and dependability. While Clyde was in jail, she visited him often as much as several times a day.

Late on the evening of March 11, 1930, after regular visiting hours, she persuaded the jailer to let her see Clyde just one more time before she had to return to Dallas. A little later that same evening, Clyde Barrow and two fellow prisoners engineered an astonishing jailbreak. The instrument of persuasion was a pistol in the hand of Clyde Barrow. Faithful Bonnie had been the only person to visit him that day, and the logical assumption, later verified, was that Bonnie had secreted the gun on her person, and had managed to pass it to Clyde. The escaped prisoners were apprehended a week later in Middletown, Ohio, but not before they had committed several robberies. They were quickly identified by fingerprints and returned to Waco. On April 21, 1930, Clyde Barrow was sentenced to a term of fourteen years in the Huntsville Penitentiary.

Roy Thornton, the forgotten man, was in the same penitentiary, but he and Clyde never became acquainted.

For a time, Clyde and Bonnie carried on a voluminous and torrid correspondence, addressing each other as husband and wife in order to facilitate passage by censor. One newspaper related that Mrs. Parker was very fond of Clyde, and encouraged Bonnie in the correspondence. In any event, Bonnie tired of this long range companionship, and the letter writing ceased.

During the next two years, she worked at several jobs; one was selling cosmetics, at which her fine complexion was a compelling asset. She had many boyfriends. One of her most frequent escorts was a detective on the Dallas police force.

On January 27, 1932, Governor Ross Sterling granted Clyde Barrow a general parole, after he had served two years and four months of his fourteen year sentence; the parole to become effective the following month of February.

Although Clyde had a long criminal record, the Governor was acting strictly in conformity with established procedures. Then, as now, prison facilities were inadequate to accommodate the endless waiting line of sentenced convicts. There was, and usually is, a backlog of prisoners in county jails awaiting admittance to the State System. Consequently, there is always considerable pressure both by relatives and by prison officials to parole those who have a record of "good behavior." The State Pardon Board and all trial officers unanimously recommended Clyde's parole. The petition for clemency disclosed that Barrow had been sent up from McLennan County on March 24, 1930, for burglary, theft of more than fifty dollars, and theft from person—a total of eight counts—to all of which he had pleaded guilty. His prison record was declared "clear," although it was stated that he and William Turner had escaped jail in Waco, Texas, and had been recaptured. The Board's letter continued that he "was only eighteen when he got into trouble," and "that he will support his mother." Prison official, W.J. Holt, wrote "he is a young fellow of nice appearance and has plenty of sense to make a good citizen." His prison record shows him to have been "blond with blue eyes, nice appearance, temperate habits, common school education, weight 127 pounds, height 5 feet 5 inches."

Clyde was barely twenty when he entered prison, and he would grow about three inches more before his death. And although many unflattering epithets were used to describe him, there is no doubt that he had more than average good looks. He was meticulous in person and dress, even when he was constantly in flight, and this took some doing. A slight pugnacity in his features was relieved by dimples in his cheeks, which appeared with his slightest smile. A photograph of him taken a few months before his death showed him in a well-fitting suit, with neatly pressed trousers, carefully tied cravat, and snap brim hat. (More than three decades later, any young man looking exactly like Clyde Barrow, and wearing the identical clothing, would have passed as a representative young American with a good, steady job.) He dyed his hair several times, but that was probably for the purpose of preventing an easy recognition or identification.

During the time that Clyde was in the Eastham Prison Farm, he suffered the loss of his left large toe. In May, 1934, a Fort Worth newspaper related that the toe had been chopped off in 1932 by a fellow convict. A diligent reporter discovered that one James McCoy was in the Tarrant County jail, preparatory to taking a "post-graduate course" at Huntsville prison. McCoy, who had been at the Eastham Prison Farm at the time of the amputation, contributed the following story:

"We were working like mad, chopping wood, two men to a log. We had an awful tough guard. Barrow was working with Hill, a life-termer. All of a sudden, Barrow yelled that his foot was cut. The guard come running up and took off his shoe. Clyde was sent to the main hospital, and was walking on crutches when he got paroled. I got the impression that it was an accident, but often convicts got someone to maim them to avoid work. Clyde was a good worker, though."

Clyde Barrow, with his wild and lawless spirit, must have been completely miserable at the prison farm. Bonnie had quit writing to him, and the years ahead seemed long and hard. It is possible that his misery might have reached such pitch that he persuaded Hill to maim him, but considering his pride and the care of his person, this is difficult to believe. Optimists cherish a fond delusion that transgressors of the law may be rehabilitated in prison. It does not happen very often. Clyde entered the penitentiary with a long record of burglaries and thefts. He came out a hardened, ruthless, dangerous criminal.

He was not long in finding Bonnie. The reunion was joyous and the reconciliation complete. Clyde was still suffering from the recent amputation and he took up residence at the Parker home for his convalescence. When he recovered sufficiently, he got a job with a construction company, but the work was disagreeable and hard, and he soon quit it. A few weeks later, he, Bonnie and another man, attempted a burglary at Kaufman, a little town east of Dallas. Clyde was out of practice and bungled the job. Interrupted before the operation was completed, they fled in a stolen car but, unfortunately, got stuck in the mud and they had to continue on foot. Clyde's gallantry on this occasion did not match Bonnie's loyalty and efficiency at Waco. He escaped and she was caught. She was kept in the Kaufman jail for several weeks and released because of insufficient evidence. Exactly five days after her arrest, Clyde and Raymond Hamilton, an old friend and partner, robbed an oil company in Dallas. (Bonnie was reported to have driven the get-away car, but if, in fact, a woman did so, it could not have been Bonnie.)

A month later, Clyde committed his first murder. The victim was Mr. J.N. Bucher, who operated a prosperous store in Hillsboro. Clyde first went into the store for the purpose of, as it is known in the vernacular, "casing the joint." Mrs. Bucher was in attendance, had formerly lived in Dallas, had a son about Clyde's age, and, by a peculiar coincidence, thought she remembered having seen him with Clyde several times. Later, when Clyde, Raymond Hamilton, and two companions, returned to the store, Mr. Bucher was there alone. They made a small purchase and tendered a bill of large denomination, which, as they expected, necessitated opening the safe for change. Unexpectedly, Mr. Bucher called his wife to do so, and in the ensuing melee, Mr. Bucher was shot and killed. The trio escaped, but Mrs. Bucher subsequently identified Clyde and Hamilton from photographs.

Bonnie was not with him at the next killing. It took place August 5, 1932, near Atoka, Oklahoma. On that night, Clyde, Raymond Hamilton, and two other male companions, were cruising around when they came upon a country dance hall, where a dance was in progress. Hamilton had an irresistible love of dancing, and they stopped, either for the purpose of allowing him to enjoy himself, or to swap the car they were driving for a more suitable one.

After they drove into the parking area, they had some minutes of earnest discussion, then got out of their car and into another one. Unknown to them, Sheriff Maxwell and his deputy, Eugene Moore, were standing outside the dance hall, and had observed them. When they saw them get into the second car, the officers walked over to investigate. In the shooting which followed, the deputy was killed immediately, and the Sheriff died later of his wounds.

The killers ran back to their own car, which had Texas license plates on it, and sped off. Some of the young men at the dance gave ineffective chase.

In the course of the escape, more than half-a-dozen car swappings were managed by the fugitives. Clyde and Hamilton were not recognized at the time, but within a short while abandoned stolen cars marked the trail and fingerprints did the rest. The last stolen car was found abandoned at Grandview, some thirty miles south of Dallas. The killers, probably by then in more than one car, must have been met by a confederate, or doubled back to Dallas in still another automobile.

On November 27, 1932, Governor Ross Sterling revoked the parole which he had granted Clyde Barrow the preceding January. A long list of Clyde's known crimes was attached to the revocation. It included three murders, numerous robberies with firearms, felonious assaults, and thefts. Clyde was now fair game for all peace officers. When confronted by one or more of them, his future policy would be either to shoot or kidnap, depending upon the circumstances and his fancy at the time.

There is a popular belief of doubtful validity that police are more than usually active and diligent in apprehending the killer of one of their own. It is quite true, though, that as time went on, there were compelling reasons for very special efforts to catch Clyde Barrow. He had not only killed or kidnapped two dozen or more of them, but frequently made them appear to be hopelessly incompetent.

Even when completely surrounded, and outnumbered by elaborately equipped and prepared groups of officers, he and Bonnie, usually with one or more companions, made miraculous escapes—shooting their way out and leaving the police to count their dead and wounded.

Bonnie had become known as "Clyde's girl," but as yet she had not been directly involved in any of his violent crimes. He taught her proficiency in handling firearms of all sorts, but he was frequently away with some of his partners, and Bonnie was at her mother's home. After the shooting of the officers at Atoka, the die was cast. One morning Bonnie told her mother that she was going to ride around with Clyde for a little while. Mrs. Parker did not see her again for more than a year.

And now began the Great Chase. For the next two years, Clyde and Bonnie, usually with companions, blazed a gory trail of crime and violence through Illinois, Missouri, Kansas, Arkansas, Oklahoma, Colorado, New Mexico, Louisiana, and Texas. It was certainly one of the greatest man hunts in the history of American crime; a cat and mouse affair sometimes played in reverse. Various newspapers referred to it as "Odyssey of Crime," "Crimson Voyage," "Ride of Death," and other leads of equally sensational nature. (There is indisputable evidence that Clyde and Bonnie both were eager readers of the news of themselves, as well as of the cheaper sensational magazine exploits of others.)

They liked company, even the enforced association of kidnapped officers; but their usual associates were Buck and his wife, Raymond Hamilton, the Clause brothers, W.D. Jones, and Henry Methvin. The last two were of the type known as "trigger happy." As time went on, these desperado companions were either killed or imprisoned, and at the end, Clyde and Bonnie were quite alone.

The modus operandi required automobiles and guns—guns of every description, from pistols to machine guns. Clyde and Bonnie were experts in the use of them.

Clyde was an able and daring driver: when on the run it was not unusual for him to drive more than a thousand miles in one day, and after committing a crime at one place, he could be at what seemed to be an impossibly distant one in an impossibly short length of time. He must have possessed unusual powers of orientation; he seemed to know all the main roads as well as the back roads and by-roads, which he used frequently. But even with his admitted ability as a driver, it was inevitable, considering his speedy driving and the tremendous amount of it, that he should have frequent accidents. When these did happen, he would take the least damaged and most serviceable car, leaving the other with the hapless victim. Even when he was going no place in particular, he was going in a hurry. In a way, he was like some frantic animal, emerging from his lair and dashing madly about the country, until falling exhausted in another hiding place.

It is not the purpose of this book to detail all the crimes actually committed by Clyde and Bonnie during those harrowing two years, because they all followed the same general pattern.

One of their early adventures near Wharton, Texas, illustrates the quick thinking of which they were capable in extremity and under fire. For a while, they were almost constantly on the road and their living expenses must have been high; gasoline alone constituting a sizable item. These expenses, of course, were met by proceeds from burglaries and the occasional "knocking over" of a filling station, usually on a country road. Frequently, they would reverse directions in entering or leaving a filling station; sometimes one of them would wait at a discreet distance while the job was being done, for the purpose of confusing officers.

They had been located at Carlsbad, New Mexico, through identification of a stolen car in which Clyde, Bonnie, and Raymond Hamilton were riding. By this time, officers had acquired a genuine respect, if not fear, for the prowess of the bandits, and elaborate preparations were made to ambush them at a bridge across the Colorado River, near Wharton, Texas. The trio had acquired a second car, which they probably intended to sell to an unsuspecting or unscrupulous purchaser, (a practice which they would soon abandon as cumbersome and dangerous). As the trio approached the bridge, they were met by a veritable hail of bullets from the officers who had made the mistake of taking their position on the opposite side. Clyde, Bonnie and Raymond escaped by the simple process of stalling one car across the bridge, after which they turned and fled in the other car before the officers could remove the barrier and pursue.

A little while later, they transferred their activities to the Middle West, ranging through Michigan, Illinois and Missouri, and it was during that time that they lost Raymond Hamilton for a while. His father lived in Michigan, and Raymond left his colleagues for an intended short visit, in the role of prodigal son. But Raymond's weakness for girls and dancing led to his undoing. He became acquainted with a dancehall Delilah to whom he talked unguardedly and too much. The treacherous young woman, doubtless for a consideration, put the finger on him for the police. He was extradited to Texas, and for his various crimes, including the Bucher slaying at Hillsboro, received a hypothetical penitentiary sentence of two hundred and sixty years.

Although Clyde gathered other companions and kindred spirits as a result of his extensive acquaintance with the underworld during his own prison sojourn, Raymond Hamilton was one of his favorites and he missed him sorely. Perhaps a combination of this loneliness and the holiday homing instinct caused him and Bonnie to return to Dallas.

On New Year's Eve of 1932, Odell Chandless, an ex-convict friend of Clyde's, had robbed the bank at Grapevine, Texas. Chandless had a lady friend at Dallas. Clyde knew her too, and he figured Chandless would make his way to her house for a temporary hiding place. He decided to pay a friendly social call.

But the police had the same idea about Chandless and had arranged an elaborate stake-out at her home. The lady, meanwhile, had departed on a holiday visit to another friend and admirer—none other than Raymond Hamilton—in residence at Huntsville Prison. A dozen armed deputies were secreted in various spots in and around the house.

On the night of January 6, 1933, Clyde, Bonnie and W.D. Jones, whom Clyde had picked up as running mate about that time, drove up to the dark house. With engine running, lights on, and Bonnie at the wheel, Clyde knocked discreetly on the front door. It was opened by young Deputy Malcolm Davis. Clyde shot and killed him instantly. He ran to the car and all three escaped. They reputedly drove to Oklahoma and on to Missouri, with their usual speed.

Confrontation of Clyde and Bonnie by an officer was not always fatal. Occasionally, it resulted in a display of sarcastic, mocking humor. Such an instance occurred a little later in the month, at Springfield, Missouri. Motorcycle Officer Thomas Persell succeeded in stopping a speeding car on the outskirts of the city. In it, were Clyde, Bonnie and another man. As Officer Persell prepared to issue a speeding ticket, the surprised man was expertly frisked of his gun and deposited on the floor in the back of the car, at the feet of W.D. Jones, who was the backseat rider. The mystery of the abandoned motorcycle and the vanished officer was the sensation of Springfield, until the next day when, after his unexpected ride, the embarrassed policeman reported by telephone from a small town several hundred miles distant.

Buck Barrow, Clyde's highly esteemed brother and mentor, was released from the penitentiary on March 22,

1933. He and his wife, Blanche, joined Clyde, Bonnie and W.D. Jones in Joplin, Missouri soon thereafter. Abandoning the comparative safety of the open road and secret hideouts, they rented quarters in Joplin to enjoy the comforts of middle-class ease. It was a great mistake. The place they rented was known as a garage-apartment, which provided parking space for automobiles on the ground floor and living accomodations above. Here they must have rested for a while. But the identities of the residents were discovered by the police and, this time, the police made preparations which they thought would surely result in the capture of the fugitives.

Early in the morning, an armed detachment surrounded the place, and a pitched battle took place. Clyde and Jones were armed with machine guns, and although bullets made a shambles of the garage and living quarters, the gun and pistols of the police could not match the barrage of fire laid down by Clyde and W.D. Jones. Bonnie, too, lent a helping hand, but brother Buck was not an experienced gunman and Blanche became hysterical.

The officers had blocked the drive with an automobile, and even though Clyde and Jones were both wounded, they managed to push it aside in a heavy rain of bullets, get Buck and Bonnie into their own car and take off, picking up the frightened, fleeing Blanche who had run some distance down the street. Clyde's machine gun had wrought havoc with the attacking law forces. Several dead, dying and wounded officers were the toll.

In their haste, the bandits left behind some highly interesting items, among them some of Bonnie's literary efforts, including a long poem entitled "Suicide Sal."

It details the story of an innocent country girl who came to town, fell in love with a deceitful gangster, and was betrayed by him. The scoundrel lured her into helping him in a bank robbery, escaped with the loot, allowed her to be captured, and then took another paramour. Bonnie must have fancied herself as the basely betrayed heroine, and the literary merits of the effort may be judged by a few lines:

"Now Sal was a gal of rare beauty,
Though her features were coarse and tough . . ."
the epic begins. And Sal begins to tell her story:
"Then I left my old home for the city
To play in its mad dizzy whirl,
Not knowing how little of pity
It holds for a country girl."

Even more interesting were photographs and undeveloped film left by the quintet. One of them showed Bonnie with a big, black cigar in her mouth, leaning against an automobile, nonchalantly dangling a large pistol from one hand. Newspapers pounced on the picture with great glee, conferring on Bonnie the enduring tag "Cigar-smoking Gun Moll." And, to add to Officer Persell's acute embarrassment, the pistol Bonnie inelegantly dangled was identified as his.

Bonnie was a cigarette smoker; she did not really smoke cigars. The picture was one of those supposedly comic snapshots which even the most shy among us sometimes cooperate in making.

Several robberies in this general locality were charged to the Barrow band in the weeks following, but the only authenticated effort took place at Okabena, Minnesota on May 16, 1933, where the local bank was robbed in front of its dazed and unbelieving customers and employees.

Buck and Blanche Barrow were not with Clyde when his usual degree of prescience deserted him on June 8, 1933, near Wellington, Texas. It was there he attempted to drive across a ravine by way of a bridge which had disappeared. The car catapulted across, caught fire and burned Bonnie severely. Clyde and W.D. Jones carried Bonnie and some of their guns to a nearby farmhouse, where the women there tried to take care of Bonnie's painful injuries. One of the men in the farmhouse decided that Bonnie's burns were serious enough to need a doctor's attention, but Clyde identified himself and, at gun point, ordered everyone to remain in the house. When a woman suddenly entered the room at which W.D. Jones guarded the door, he shot her in the hand.

For once, Clyde was without transportation, and there was none in sight. Eventually, one of the captives escaped and Clyde realized that he would lead the law back. With his extraordinary ability to turn adverse circumstance to his benefit, he instructed all his captives to remain inside, while he and W.D. Jones hid in the yard outside. When the Sheriff and City Marshal arrived, Clyde and Jones surprised and disarmed them, shackling them with their own handcuffs. Then, putting the sheriff on the backseat of the police car, with Bonnie carefully propped in the middle, between the officer and W.D. Jones, and the City Marshal in the front seat beside Clyde, they headed for Oklahoma. After two days of backroad flight, the officers were put out, unharmed but afoot, and were thanked for being so kind and attentive to the suffering Bonnie. The officers, if not particularly thrilled by the ride, were grateful and thankful for having been freed.

Contact was made again with Buck and Blanche, and a safe hideout was found in Arkansas, where Bonnie could rest and recover from her burns. It was still necessary for the "men of the family" to bring home the bacon, most of which, appropriately enough, was provided by robbing larger cash grocery stores, the forerunners of today's supermarkets. After one such robbery, the City Marshal of Alma, Arkansas, reading a description of Buck and Clyde, recognized them as the men who had carried him into the Alma Bank a few days before, tied him up, and then robbed the bank. Accordingly, he started out with a deputy to catch them. It was his misfortune that he succeeded in encountering them, and the result was a bullet hole through his heart. The deputy escaped.

When Bonnie recovered sufficiently to be able to travel, they drove up through Iowa, stopping en route to rob several filling stations, where Bonnie was identified by the bandages she still wore.

Finally they stopped at a tourist camp outside Platte City, Missouri, where they took a double cabin. By this time, the Barrow Gang had become so dangerous and feared that travellers were frightened by just the possibility of encountering them or being mistaken for them. Newspapers, placards, and bulletins kept the public acutely aware of the sudden danger and death which might be met on the highways. Platte City was a small town and all visitors attracted attention, including those who stopped at the Red Crown Tourist Camp. Clyde, Bonnie, Buck, Blanche and Jones were careful not to be seen together. Bonnie still needed bandages and dressings for her burns, and these were bought for her at the local drugstore. This became known, by way of small-town gossip. Occasionally, one of the gang would buy five lunches or dinners to take out at the few cafes or restaurants, and this too was observed. Newspapers from the larger towns were circulated in Platte City, and before long, the rumors had begun that the five strangers at the Red Crown were members of the Barrow Gang.

This time, peace officers decided that plans would be laid with meticulous care to prevent any possible slip. The Sheriff at Kansas City, Missouri was called for help, and equipment of the attacking force this time would include machine guns and an armored car. After the plans and arrangements were checked and rechecked, two of the officers, with drawn pistols, approached the door of Clyde's cabin. Clyde Barrow, always alert, recognized the first premonitory knock for what it was and realized what was going to happen. The intensity and violence of this battle far exceeded that of the battle at Joplin. A bullet accidentally activated the siren on the armored motor car, and it added its hoarse and penetrating sound to the general confusion. Clyde's car was parked between the rooms of the double cabin. Once again, as at Joplin, he managed to get Buck, who had been seriously wounded, and Blanche, who had been wounded as well, the still ailing Bonnie, and W.D. Jones and himself into the car and make his escape. The officers had set up road blocks at the probable points Clyde would pass if he managed to escape, but the crafty Clyde never appeared at any of them.

For several days they must have camped out with the two wounded Barrows and the crippled Bonnie. However, they were trailed to a wooded point near Dexter, Iowa, and a large posse attacked them. Buck was shot several times again, even more seriously. Bonnie, Clyde and Jones also received wounds, and in the darkness made a miraculous escape. Blanche either refused or was unable to leave the fatally wounded Buck. He died a few days later, July 29, 1933, in a hospital in Perry, Iowa. Exactly how the other three made their incredible escape must remain sheer mystery.

Although all were suffering from serious injuries, Clyde stole another automobile and was seen a short time later in Denison, Iowa, where he bought a hypodermic syringe and medicine, apparently for Bonnie.

Again, the fugitives had to rest and recover from their wounds. It was becoming less difficult for the law officers to trace their movements. They must have headed back to Texas; in any case, in some secret retreat, they managed a considerable period of rest and relaxation. But soon they were to realize, for the first time, that complete loyalty from associates, or even family, could no longer be taken for granted.

On November 26, 1933, Sheriff Smoot Schmid of Dallas County prepared an ambuscade near a place where Clyde and Bonnie were rumored to have a meeting with Bonnie's mother. The tip may have come from W.D. Jones, who at that time was in the Dallas jail and "singing" unreservedly for the cops. Someone had to tell the sheriff, but he never revealed his source. In any case, once again, Clyde and Bonnie escaped under fire in the darkness, stealing several automobiles on their way north. Both had been wounded again.

But, without doubt, the most daring and sensational exploit was yet to come. With Buck Barrow dead, Blanche Barrow in prison, Raymond Hamilton in prison, and W.D. Jones in jail, Clyde and Bonnie were bereft of companions. On January 16, 1934, they attacked the Texas State Prison System, specifically the Eastham Prison Farm, where Raymond Hamilton was confined.

All Texas law violations are prosecuted as being "against the peace and dignity of the State of Texas." But here was a physical attack on the State itself, in the exercise of functions necessary to its existence; something more like a revolt or insurrection than a mere violation of law.

Clyde, of course, was familiar with the usual routine at Eastham from his own experience there. Even so, it is obvious that considerable planning and current information was necessary for the successful execution of this extraordinary coup. Accounts of the actual event vary considerably, but a sifting of newspaper stories provides as trustworthy an account as may be had.

"In the murky gloom of an early morning fog, today, a gang of prisoners was being marched to work at the Eastham Prison Farm, where Clyde Barrow and others, including his Gun Moll, Bonnie Parker, laid down a withering sheet of machine gun fire from ambush. Two guards were wounded and one fell and in the ensuing confusion five convicts escaped. Among them was Raymond Hamilton, Barrow's best friend and his partner in many crimes of brutality and violence. Hamilton's escape was undoubtedly the primary objective in this unprecedented and seemingly impossible attack. The other escapers (that impossible and contradictory word 'escapee' had not yet come into general use) were Joe Palmer, A.B. French, James Bybee, and Henry Methvin. A wide hunt has been instituted by prison officials and descriptions of the fugitives furnished to all law enforcement agencies."

In another story, Warden W.W. Waid commented:

"Barrow has extreme cunning and will show no quarter. He says that he will never be taken alive, and he probably will not be."

Other headlines:

"Barrow linked with twelve slayings in past two years."

"Barrow writing life history for magazine, father says . . ."

"Barrow Machine Gun Writes Bandit History"

(This story continues:)

"The blond, blue-eyed, one hundred thirty pound youth is five feet seven inches tall and is said to have been born in Dallas, in 1910. Barrow and his two consorts, Raymond Hamilton and Bonnie Parker, remain untouched. Their existence hangs on two things: a beat to the draw and death-defying automobile driving. Hamilton's control at the wheel is said to be perfect and that is the reason Barrow sprung him in the recent prison break. Barrow started his splurge of crime nine years ago."

Another article, giving particular attention to Bonnie, emanated from Dallas:

"Bonnie was once a waitress in a cheap restaurant here. Raised in the squalid flats of West Dallas, she lived next door to Clyde Barrow. Her parents were of small means and neither had much education. Until two years ago, she worked in the small restaurant near the court house. She was the sweetheart of Roy Thornton now serving a sentence in the penitentiary for burglary. When Thorton 'went up' Bonnie took up with Barrow. Thornton is said to hold vengeance and has boasted that if officers would turn him loose he could get Barrow."

Some of the details in this story were corrected a few days later:

"Bonnie married Thornton in 1931. She has a mother, brother and sister living here now. They have never been in trouble. She is now 22, weighs about 95, is 5 feet 2 and one-half inches, has reddish-auburn hair and blue-gray eyes."

This is a small part of the flood of stories in Texas and elsewhere.

The State Legislature was in session in Texas at the time of the prison attack, and the horrified law-makers immediately offered a reward of One Thousand Dollars for Clyde Barrow. There was some debate as to whether the language should include "Dead or Alive." During the discussion, Clyde was referred to as "a human rat, beyond the pale of legal procedure" and "public enemy."

For Raymond Hamilton, only Five Hundred Dollars was offered.

Barrow's victims were principally officers of the law, but some of them were citizens in all walks of life and, in some cases, their encounters were less spectacular. Tom James, a prominent Ft. Worth attorney, once had a collision with a car at night on the Dallas highway near Grand Prairie. The driver of the other car, a slender young man, jumped out, briefly and silently surveyed the damage and, noting that James' car had suffered more than his own, hopped back in and sped away. James was mollified a few minutes later when pursuing police officers arrived and informed him he had had a brush with Clyde Barrow.

Another incident took place at Ruston, Louisiana. Clyde, Bonnie and W.D. Jones felt the need for a new car. They selected one belonging to a local undertaker named D.D. Darby. Undertakers usually have nice, new shiny automobiles and Mr. Darby was no exception. His was parked outside the home of his lady friend. The couple came out the door just in time to see it being driven away.

Mr. Darby and friend gave immediate pursuit in her car. It was obvious to Clyde that his choice had the edge on speed, but he permitted Darby to follow at a safe distance until they were out in the country. Clyde suddenly turned and headed toward Darby, and now Mr. Darby, who had shown such commendable bravery, became thoroughly frightened. He too turned his car around and sought to return to the city with the lady at full speed. Clyde soon overtook them and hustled the couple into the car with him, Bonnie and Jones. He took them for a long ride, during which he revealed the identities of himself and his companions. He finally put them out in Magnolia, Arkansas, with a stern warning to the undertaker to display more prudence in dealing with the living or he might find himself very soon and very literally in the hands of a competitor.

Notwithstanding the long list of crimes which the Barrow gang is known to have commited, many unsolved robberies, burglaries and other crimes of violence were inevitably laid at their doorstep. Frequently they were "identified" in two places, hundreds of miles apart, at simultaneous moments, and one newspaper carried a cynical headline reading: "Barrow Not Blamed in This One."

A particularly atrocious crime for which they were blamed took place near Grapevine, Texas, on April 1, 1934, with the murder of two State Highway patrolmen.

On that afternoon, Patrolman Polk Ivy and E.B. Wheeler, had taken a new officer, H.D. Murphy, for his first patrol, on State Highway 114. The highway was comparatively deserted at the hour, and about four miles west of Grapevine, the officers parked their motorcycles at the roadside to engage in some target practice at thrown tin cans.

The Roanoke-Dove Road crossed the highway at a short distance ahead and the occupants of a car parked about three hundred feet from the highway were in easy sight and hearing of the officers. Patrolman Ivy rode ahead of his two collegues as they left the site. He said he noticed the parked car and thought that the occupants were two men, although he thought it strange that they were "petting." Thirty years ago, public demonstrations of affection between men and women, even husband and wife, were considered in bad taste, and any such display between men was so obnoxious as to be "against the peace and dignity of the state."

Curiosity may have killed the fabled cat, but lack of it probably saved Patrolman Ivy's life. After he had ridden a considerable distance, he looked around, he said, did not see his fellow officers and rode back. He found them both dead on the side road, apparently shot off their motorcycles.

William Schieffer, whose farm bordered the side road, claimed to have seen the entire tragedy. His statement, in brief, was to the effect that the car and its occupants had been there since ten-thirty that morning, an elapsed time of more than four hours; that when the motorcycle officers turned into the cross road and had ridden some twenty-five feet, the occupants got out of the car. One was a man about five feet six inches tall, the other a woman about five feet four inches, wearing knickers. The man grabbed a shotgun from the side of the car on the driver's side, the woman a similar weapon from her side of the car. Both of them began shooting and the officers fell without ever drawing their pistols. The murderers got back in their car, drove to the highway and disappeared.

All this occurred in Tarrant County, and the Fort Worth police took charge.

According to a newspaper story, "After five days of twisting and turning a pint whiskey bottle," (found near the scene of the crime) "Barney Finn, Superintendent of the Ft. Worth Police Identification Bureau came up with the information that on the bottom of the brown bottle he had found a print of Clyde Barrow's right hand ring finger, on the neck of the bottle was one of Henry Methvin, and a third print could not be identified. On the basis of this highly circumstantial evidence, the crime was laid to "Clyde Barrow and his cigar-smoking Gun Moll, Bonnie Parker."

There were serious flaws. The affair had few earmarks of a Barrow crime and evidence was very strong that he and Bonnie were elsewhere at the time. Without doubt, at the very hour in question, Raymond Hamilton was in Houston, stealing an automobile.

Then District Attorney Jesse Martin was never of the opinion that Clyde and Bonnie were the murderers and said that he would not have brought them to trial unless more and sufficient evidence were produced.

On the other hand, former United States Marshal, "Red" Wright was convinced that they were guilty.

Geographically, Grapevine forms the apex of a triangle with Fort Worth and Dallas, and within a radius of sixty miles is the largest concentration of population in the South. The hue and cry raised by the public was tremendous and criticism of and pressure on the police—at all levels—enormous. Something had to be done. And, to the discredit of law-enforcement authorities, something was: Mrs. Billie Mace, Bonnie's sister, was charged with the crime and thrown into the Tarrant County jail.

Newspapers everywhere continued to be filled with headline stories dealing with the notorious couple and their bold, startling crimes, and it is certain that Bonnie and Clyde read them with avid interest.

Bonnie was serious when she told one of their temporary and unwilling traveling companions that she bitterly resented being dubbed a "cigar-smoking Moll." Bonnie could swallow camels but strain at gnats, and although she participated in major crimes, her outlook was provincial and insular when it came to petty vice. It would be incorrect to assume that either of the pair drank heavily; they used intoxicants seldom and sparingly, for the simple reason that it was necessary for them to be at their best in order to be capable of their worst.

Reading her reams of publicity, Bonnie was unhappily concerned about her "public image." To be accused of smoking cigars, a masculine prerogative, was to her mind repulsively unladylike. The accusation rankled. She must have harped on it so continually that Clyde entered the field of public relations on her behalf. He wrote a letter to Mr. Amon G. Carter, publisher of the **Fort Worth Star-Telegram**. The letter was dated "7:30 P.M. April 3, 1934," and postmarked the following day at Decatur, Texas.

"Dear Mr. Carter,

The postman may not find you at home but you will get this letter just the same. And you better think, decide and make up your mind and not let your editor make another remark about Bonnie like you did the other day and called her a cigar smoking woman. Another remark about my underworld mate and I will end such men as you—mighty quick. I know where you and your reporters live . . . Bonnie and I are not married . . . and I am going to take up for her and she will take up for me."

At that time, the **Star-Telegram** regularly printed this box-notice:

NOTICE TO THE PUBLIC
ANY ERRONEOUS REFLECTION UPON THE CHARACTER, STANDING OR REPUTATION OF ANY PERSON, FIRM OR CORPORATION WHICH MAY APPEAR IN THE COLUMNS OF THIS PAPER WILL BE GLADLY CORRECTED UPON DUE NOTICE OF SAME BEING GIVEN TO THE EDITOR PERSONALLY AT THE OFFICE, SEVENTH AND TAYLOR STREETS, FORT WORTH, TEXAS."

Clyde had torn this notice from a copy of the newspaper, wrote across it "read this," put an "x" opposite the promise "be gladly corrected," and affixed it to the first page of his letter.

The rest of the letter expounded his views on society, classes in general and individuals in particular. It is a small masterpiece of illiterate pornography. The four-letter word and its variants which connote sexual intercourse appear nine times in its two and one-half pages, together with other pruriencies.

"Isn't every girl and woman in Fort Worth cigarret feign (fiend) and whore . . . men ought to abuse lots of woman because they don't respect the men in the city or country either."

He threatens "old lady Ferguson" (Governor Miriam A. Ferguson) with a dire reprisal for offering a reward for him and adds, "and let Bonnie watch me."

Several prominent men, of whose conduct he did not approve, were marked for proper chastisement, in due course, and then he continued in a chatty and more mellow vein, "say boy, can't robbers get away fast in cars these days. I'm glad this country is different from what it was when Jessy James (sic) lived here."

He relates he shot the two policemen on the Grapevine by-road because they interrupted his love-making with Bonnie (he used a different term), and wrote, "all I regret was that the third cop wasn't there while our guns were hot." He confided that "we are staying at the seven-wire pasture (meaing unknown) tonight and will drive to the Brazos River and Breckenridge tomorrow." He concludes, either darkly or cheerily: "Will be seeing you soon."

Possibly Clyde wrote or dictated another letter soon after. It was postmarked "Tulsa Okla 10 April" (year not given), addressed to "Mr. Henry Ford, Detroit, Mich," and received at Detroit April 14, 1934.

"Dear Sir:
While I still got breath in my lungs I will tell you what a dandy car you make. I have drove Fords exclusively when I could get away with one . . . the Ford has got ever other car skinned and even if my business haven't been strickly legal it don't hurt anything to tell you what a fine car you got in the V8."

Men prominent in public affairs frequently receive unsolicited letters of various sorts. Such letters may be signed correctly or falsely, or not at all, and they are answered, ignored, or dumped in the wastebasket, as circumstances warrant. Mr. Carter and Mr. Ford were nationally and internationally prominent men of extensive affairs, and we must reasonably assume neither would have retained a letter from so notorious a character without satisfactory assurance of its authenticity.

There are both slight similarities and great differences in the handwriting of the two letters. The signatures in the Carter letter (Clyde Barrow) and the Fort Worth police files of 1929 match. The Ford letter was signed "Clyde Champion Barrow" and is questionable. However, the letter may have been dictated.

His glowing testimonial could not be completely disregarded. It was used by the Dallas Ford Agency. The original letter is in the Henry Ford Museum at Dearborn, Michigan, and an enlarged reproduction of it hangs in the office of Sheriff Lon Evans of Fort Worth.

The vitality of Clyde and Bonnie was enormous, their ability to get from place to place almost incredible, but whether or not they were near Grapevine on April 1, 1934 or in Decatur on April 3, 1934, they were certainly in the Northeast corner of Oklahoma a few days later, engaged in another capricious adventure.

News of the latest event was first received from Miami, Oklahoma, although the sequence of events originated at the small town of Commerce, some thirty miles to the north. Bonnie, Clyde and another man had their car stuck in the mud. Passersby were stopped and forced at gunpoint to help extricate the car. One agile citizen managed to slip away and notify town authorities. Constable Cal Campbell and Chief of Police Percy Boyd arrived at the scene just as the car was freed. There was a gun battle and some fifteen or twenty shots were fired. The Constable was killed. Boyd received a slight scalp wound and was forced into the car with the bandits. They sped away only to become mired again about three miles further down the road. This time they were dragged free by A.N. Butterfield, a farmer, who was encouraged in his efforts by their waving guns. Butterfield did not see Boyd in the car, but he was lying on the backseat or floor, and his account of the matter, although lengthy, is worth repeating:

"The car headed over Stepp's Ford Bridge across the Neosho, west and north," related the Chief of Police. "All three of them had light complexions and one of the men appeared to have a face skin disease. I recognized Clyde and Bonnie but I was not sure of the third person. We had a wild ride north into Kansas. We drove into Fort Scott shortly before dark and bought newspapers telling of the Commerce shooting. They bought suppers and we took them into the woods to eat. We came back to town about ten o'clock at night and Clyde tried to steal a car. But he could not find one to suit him, so they drove south. Barrow and Bonnie sat in the front seat and I sat in the back with the other man who I took to be Raymond Hamilton." (He was wrong; it was Henry Methvin.)

"We drove to Chetopa, Kansas, then turned north through Bartlett, which was the only town of any size we passed through. We stopped three times during the day for gasoline. None seemed to suspect that they were filling up Clyde Barrow's gas tank. In our traveling, we used byroads mostly. We rarely took a main highway. Bonnie took the opportunity to tell how she felt about certain things. She said she wanted me to tell her public that she did not smoke cigars. She said she once had her picture taken with a cigar in her mouth and that it had gotten in the hands of a newspaper and was published. She was plenty mad about it. The picture was made from an undeveloped film found in a hideout near Joplin, Missouri, from which the Barrow gang escaped after killing two officers. Bonnie had a soft spot in her heart for white rabbits. She carried one in a box at her side and stroked it as they tore through the countryside. Barrow acted like he owned the earth. He thinks quite a lot about himself—cocky. The other fellow is much like Barrow but Barrow is king pin. Barrow denied he and his followers were responsible for the recent slaying of two officers near Grapevine, Texas. They carried a regular arsenal. I counted three machine guns, two sawed-off shotguns and a number of pistols. And plenty of ammunition! Much of Friday afternoon we spent traveling on side roads between Fort Scott and Pittsburg. No one seemed to recognize us or even be looking for us—even in Fort Scott. Clyde drove all the time. The car was a new one, only three thousand miles on it. I saw the speedometer hit 90 several times. They said I could tell anything as long as it was true. They treated me fine. The wound in the back of my head was given first aid treatment and they told me to see a doctor right away when they let me out. They even gave me a good clean shirt."

Crimes of violence are usually sudden and swift. Spectators and participants see them from different viewpoints and are likely to give conflicting stories. There is no reason to doubt the story of Chief Percy Boyd in its essential points. He was in the line of fire, and may be forgiven for having stated that fifty or sixty shots were fired at Commerce. Other spectators guessed the number as less than one-fourth of his count. His statement does present a strange picture of the headlong flights of Clyde Barrow and Bonnie Parker and their senseless, directionless wanderings.

As might be expected, after Hamilton's deliverance from the penitentiary, Clyde and he got together to pull a few jobs. But for some reason, the partnership didn't last this time and it was Henry Methvin who replaced Hamilton as the faithful companion.

The headlines continued.

BANDIT AND MOLL CHARGED IN DOUBLE SLAYING.

BARROW BONNIE HUNT GOES ON
SHERIFF OPENS FUNDS FOR REWARDS
REWARD OF $3615 FOR SLAYERS
BARROW AND BONNIE BELIEVED IN FORT WORTH
OFFICERS CERTAIN IT WAS CLYDE AND BONNIE
$1500 BOUNTY PUT ON KILLS.
But events were moving to their inevitable conclusion. And it happened on the gravel road eighteen miles from Arcadia, Louisiana, on May 23, 1934.

With the unerring speed and precision of vultures, on that morning several hundred people gathered around the automobile and its dead passengers. Souvenir hunters went to work immediately: a handbag disappeared, pieces of Bonnie's clothing were snipped off, **every shred of broken glass was picked up from the road, and one man tried to complete the severance of Clyde's ear in order to preserve it in alcohol.**

The news was flashed to the world.

In Washington, Representative Kleburg told Congress and the nation that Texas was to be congratulated for wiping out the Number One Public Enemy.

At Austin, the cost to the public of their depredations was estimated in the millions.

Roy Thornton, at Reprive Prison Farm, (whence he had attempted escape two months prior to that), stated: "I haven't seen Bonnie since 1931. I'm no snitcher. But I'm glad they went like that. It was better than getting caught. That's all."

The shattered gray sedan with its riddled occupants remained on the road for several hours before being towed into Arcadia and placed in a wire fence at the jail. Thousands of people came to view it throughout the day and night and to mill around the establishment where the bodies had been taken.

The most highly prized and negotiable trophy was a bullet taken from either body. These became commonplace since there was a total of ninety.

Newspapers printed all the bloody details. Both bodies were horribly mangled and it will be perhaps suficient to record that Clyde's body had to be embalmed in sections.

Buster Parker appeared in Arcadia with a Dallas undertaker. Both families had prudently maintained burial insurance policies.

"The dirty dogs did it from ambush," Buster cried. "Did you see her? Wasn't it pitiful? Shot and shot again . . . ."

And he defended his other sister, Billie Mace, who was being held in the Tarrant County jail for what had come to be called "The Easter Sunday Murders," at Grapevine.

"The law just hounds us," he declared bitterly. And there was justification for his complaint. The Parker family had done nothing worse than shelter and protect daughter and sister, technically a violation of the law, but no more than the average person would have done under similar circumstances.

On the same day that Buster Parker went east to bring back the body of his dead sister, Mrs. Parker came west to Fort Worth to visit her daughter, Billie. Most of the newspaper stories had been written in unrestrained hyperbole, which was characteristic of the period, but this event was handled by a Fort Worth newspaper in a direct and succinct manner which created a great deal of sympathy for the mother grieving over the death of one daughter and trying to help and comfort another in trouble.

By this time (at least for the time being) Farmer Schieffer had made up his mind, and identified Billie Mace and Raymond Hamilton as the woman and man whom he had seen in the car that fatal Easter Sunday.

Now that the protagonists in this incredible drama were dead, publicity and attention turned for a while to the avenging furies which had felled them. We speak of the law-enforcement authorities. Their stories, like others concerning Clyde and Bonnie, were a mixture of truth, half-truth and lies. Typical of the latter was one a Louisiana officer told his Governor. (He was one of the ambush party).

As the car approached at a speed of 85 miles per hour, "some of the officers quickly walked into the road and called for a halt."

An officer from Bienville Parish stated:

"I've been working on the case about six weeks. Barrow did not drive into his death-trap at 85 miles per hour. Last night I received a tip they would be on the Jamestown-Sailes road this morning. So I drove out and picked a place . . . a natural barricade at the top of a little hill. Alcorn personally knew Clyde and Bonnie and sighted them a quarter mile away. When they got a hundred yards away coming up grade he said, 'That's them, boys.' The car, meeting a truck slowed down . . . we hollered to Barrow to halt—we wanted to give them a chance. They went for their guns and we let them have it. More than a hundred and fifty shots were fired breast-high and both of them were shot to pieces. The outside door moulding looked like the inside of a lemon grater."

Parts of this story were true, but it was as full of holes as the door moulding. In this embarrassing situation, it became necessary for the usually reticent Captain Frank Hamer to be the official spokesman. The burly Captain, a Texas Ranger, had travelled more than 15,000 miles trailing Clyde and Bonnie, and had always arrived a little too late. This time, with two Dallas deputy sheriffs, a Texas Highway Patrolman and two officers of Bienville Parish, Louisiana, he finally brought the hunt to an end.

His first statement:

"I never discuss a case I'm working on before, during and after its conclusion."

Unfortunately for the Captain, he later reconsidered and this was his second statement:

"I hated to bust a cap on a woman, especially when she was sitting down. However, if it hadn't been her it would have been us. Bonnie got in the way of bullets aimed at Clyde Barrow. When I fired I thought about the way she helped kill those two patrolmen at Grapevine, how she was in on the murder of nine officers in Missouri, Oklahoma, Arkansas and Texas. A woman of that kind has something like that coming to her. We expected the Barrow car at exactly 9:27 in the morning; it came at 9:15. I got a tip at my hotel Monday night that all was set . . . . About 7:30 Sunday night, Clyde and Bonnie drove out the highway looking for a certain kind of signboard. They found the signboard but there wasn't any message under it. The information they expected hadn't come and they sat there all night waiting for the messenger. Then they returned to Arcadia and started out the Gibsland road looking for a second board. They found us instead. Clyde was driving about thirty miles per hour. I gave them a chance to stop but they didn't, so we gave them the same medicine they had given others. The first shots took away part of Bonnie Parker's face. . . . She screamed like a panther. Clyde was driving with stocking feet and didn't die with his boots on. I started working on this case February 10th and interviewed countless denizens of the underword."

The Captain paused.

"Barrow did not make many contacts but when he made them they stuck by him."

In response to a direct question, the Captain continued:

"Why did I pick this neighborhood? A study in human nature! Barrow was hot everywhere except Louisiana. So they came here. I tell you, Barrow was the smartest of them all. Dillinger and the rest of that crowd don't rate knee-high with him. He is the most elusive and smartest man I ever tracked."

Newspaper reporters are persistent and tenacious. The

Captain's mysterious allusions and contradictions somewhat tarnished his reputation. It would have been better if he had begun with the truth, since he had to tell it later.

It was Henry Methvin who, with the promise of a full pardon, had lured Clyde and Bonnie to their deaths.

After more criminal activity he was decapitated at Coushatta, Louisiana, while crawling under a moving freight train.

The excitement at Arcadia was nothing compared to the demonstrations in Dallas when the bodies of Clyde and Bonnie were brought there. The distress and anguish of the relatives were impressive. They had lived in fear for more than two years. With people of their class and in their era, exhibitions of grief were considered appropriate; lack of them would have been thought callous indifference. In describing the family's demonstrations of grief, writers and correspondents pulled out all the stops.

Mrs. Parker had refused to have a joint funeral for Bonnie and Clyde, and intended having a private ceremony for Bonnie at her home. When this became known, thousands of people gathered outside the house, breaking fences, trampling shrubbery and otherwise creating havoc. The disturbances were so fantastic that plans were changed.

The undertaking establishment in Dallas was besieged by the public as soon as the bodies arrived, and police had to be called. When the morticians had finished, the bodies were laid out for the customary viewing by relatives and friends. Again, thousands of people, in single file, prodded by police, gaped. The shocked relatives asked the undertakers to close their doors and it required hundreds of policemen to restrain the frenzied, disappointed latecomers.

Clyde Barrow was buried first. A Reverend Andrews volunteered his services and an account of the rites reads, in part, as follows:

"BARROW LAID TO REST NEAR HIS OLD HOME

"In the old French Cemetery, among tall blue larkspur

and fallen headstones, souvenir hunters snatched roses, gladioli and peonies from Clyde Barrow's grave as his aged mother was led wailing from the grave. For two days and nights, crowds had fought for a chance for a last look at the Dallas youth whose name in five years had come to send a streak of terror across the Middle West as peace officers, one after another, died in a futile attempt to stop him. A quartet sang 'The Old Rugged Cross' and 'Beautiful Isle of Somewhere.' Then the procession rolled slowly to the grave. The press of the crowd at the cemetery was so great that an aunt and young woman cousin of the dead outlaw fainted. An airplane flew overhead and dropped a spray of gladioli on which was a card reading 'From a Flier Friend.'

As for the "press of the crowd," it was more than that. Traffic was blocked in all directions and within a few minutes after the ceremonies were completed, the grave was completely stripped of flowers.

Bonnie's funeral was held the following day. The crowds, perhaps ashamed of the outrageous demonstrations of the preceding day, were more orderly but no less curious. A minister of the Full Gospel Church conducted the services, which were held in the chapel of the funeral home. Although the attendance was supposedly limited to members of the family, more than one hundred and fifty people crowded into the small chapel while mobs outside had to be restrained by the police with stretched ropes. Billie Mace was allowed to attend in custody of a deputy sheriff. She swooned when she saw the poor, patched-up body of her sister.

Hysterics were general. One of the wreaths on the casket was marked with a card: "Dallas Newsboys to Bonnie Parker." Flashlights popped and news cameras ground, as the procession, guided by motorcycle police, took the route to Fishtrap Cemetery, a mile from Clyde's last resting place. This time the headline was:

"LAW SHE DESPISED LEADS BONNIE PARKER TO GRAVE."

Properly speaking, the story of Clyde and Bonnie ends here. But there are a few loose ends. On June 14, 1934, Judge George Hosey dismissed the charges against Mrs. Billie Mace.

A Mr. D.U. McCabe, of Fort Worth, proferred bronze plaques for the graves of Clyde and Bonnie. McCabe was a mechanic and foundry foreman for a refining company, whose hobby was bronze work. Mrs. Parker accepted the offer. She said she wanted to use some of Bonnie's poetry on it, but couldn't find anything appropriate.

"She left a piece of paper with a verse on it," said Mr. McCabe, "and said for me to go ahead and make the plaque. I do not know the author of the verse. This is the way it reads:

BONNIE PARKER
October 1, 1910—May 23, 1934
As the flowers are made all the sweeter
By the sunshine and the dew
So this old world is made sweeter
By the lives of folks like you."

BONNIE PARKER in person with cigar and Clyde's car.

CLYDE CHAMPION BARROW Dallas A 8 4316 29 M 9
@ Jack Hale @ Elvin Williams 26 U 00 6
(White)

Age 22(1932) Ht.5-7 BF. Wt.125. Hair D.Blonde(reddish) Eyes Hazel.
Com.Lt. Occ.None. Res.West Dallas,Dallas,Tex. Nat.Ellis Co.Texas.

12-3-26	Arr.Dallas,Texas;Auto Theft.
3-25-32	Wanted Dallas,Texas;Robbery by Fire Arms and Burglary.
4-30-32	Wanted Hillsboro,Texas;Murder and Robbery by Fire Arms.
5-12-32	Wanted Lufkin,Texas;Robbery by Fire Arms.
8-1-32	Wanted Dallas,Texas;Robbery by Fire Arms.
8-5-32	Wanted Atoka,Okla;Murder and Assault to Murder.
8-30-32	Wanted Wharton County Texas for Assault to Murder.
10-8-32	Wanted Abilene,Texas;Robbery by Fire Arms.

This man is very dangerous and extreme care should be taken when arresting him.

CLYDE C. BARROW
(Companion of
Raymond Hamilton,
also wanted)

NAME Clyde Champion Barrow NO. 4316 CLASS 29 M 9 MALE
Jack Hale 26 U 00 6
(White)

Age 18 (1928) Height 5-6 3/4; Weight 132; Build M Slender; Hair
Lt Ch; Eyes Ch; Complexion Fair; Occupation Trimmer; Nativity
Texas; Residence Dallas, Texas-West Dallas, Route 8, Box 6.

II. Tat Anchor; shield and Initials "U.S.N." elb ft.
III. Small flesh mole at 1/2 abv center rt brow.

Arrested 2-22-1928 by James-Chapple company #3131, J. L. Moore,
chg. Investigation-General Principles.
Record:- As same name #6048 Dallas, Texas 12-3-1926, chg. Auto
Theft.
Montgomery-Finn.

Clyde Barrow

DEPARTMENT OF POLICE, FORT WORTH, TEXAS

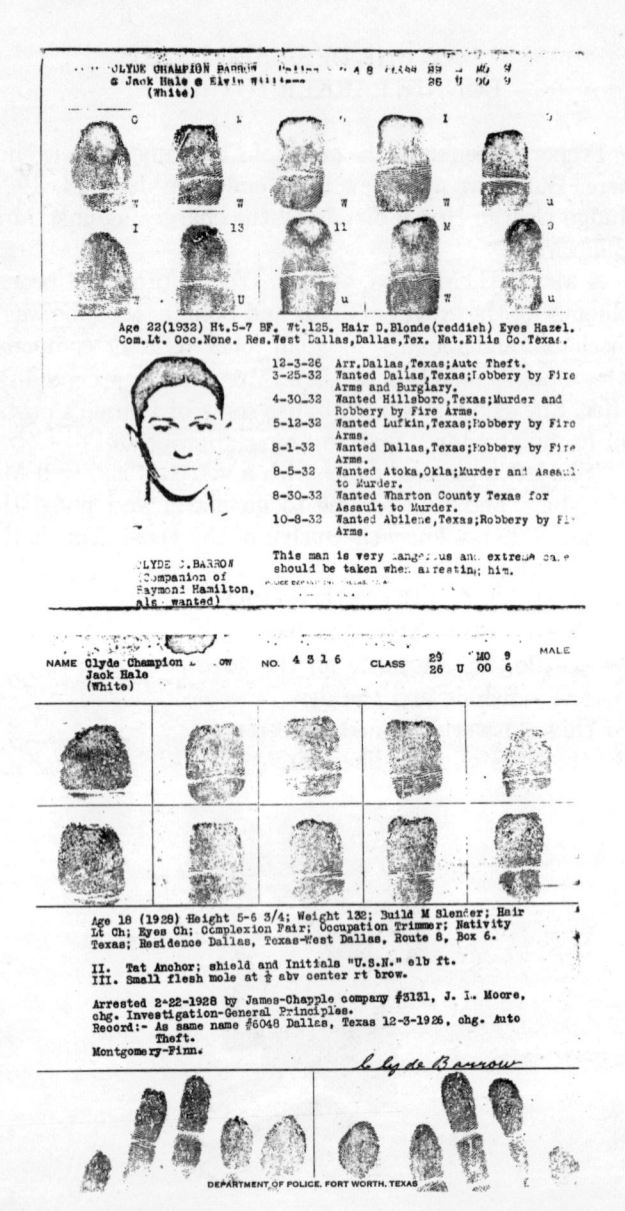

POLICE RECORDS for Clyde Barrow and Bonnie Parker.

EPILOGUE

In 1958, "The Bonnie Parker Story" starring Dorothy Provine and Jack Hogan came and went without any appreciable notice.

In 1967, another movie, based on the lives of the almost forgotten couple was made, entitled "Bonnie and Clyde," transposing the usual juxtaposition of the names.

It was a low-budget picture and only one person connected with it, its male star and producer, Warren Beatty, was well-known. The female lead was played by Faye Dunaway. The location shots were filmed in Dallas.

The response of the public to the picture was immediate and overwhelming. This sleeper made movie history and is probably among the all-time leaders in gross profits. Millions have seen it, many more than once, and today it is still being shown at small theatres and drive-ins and on television.

There was, as a result, an assortment of effects in entertainment, literature, and fashion.

The film followed not the facts surrounding the notorious pair, but what was perceived by Bonnie Parker as set down by her in her "ballad." It was a deliberately romanticized adventure, made to entertain rather than to inform or moralize. Clyde and Bonnie were not criminals so much as heroes in this version.

But the real reason for its success was perhaps that it was psychologically relevant to the audience and the time. Half or more of our population is under twenty-five years old. From it comes the vast majority of movie goers. It has always been typical of youth to protest against an apparently harsh, self-righteous, authoritarian discipline. From somewhat different motivation, Clyde and Bonnie were the foremost practitioners of protest in their day, supreme activists one might say. In the current lingo, member of the audience could relate to Clyde and Bonnie.

That film was among the first in the field of explicit sexual antics, and no doubt this was a factor in its success. With motion pictures now considered an art form, it would please Bonnie and Clyde mightily to know that they contributed to a conspicuous trend in contemporary culture.

Their ghosts must relish even more the fact that the July 19, 1973 issue of the prestigious Wall Street Journal featured a story of the fantastic auction price on the bullet-riddled 1943 Ford in which they were riding when killed. Another press report claimed that the seller had realized over a million dollars in exhibition fees and that the new buyer would continue this profitable activity at $2.50 per look. The Aug. 13, 1973 issue of Time revealed that the Ford finally sold for $175,000.00 which made it "the most expensive used car in history, dearer even than Hitler's Mercedes which went for $153,000.00 last January."

This would bolster any ego, even theirs.

PART

2

John Wesley

Hardin

JOHN WESLEY HARDIN

JOHN WESLEY HARDIN
1853-1895

John Wesley Hardin shot and killed forty men before his twenty-fifth birthday. Except for comparable military exploits in time of war, Hardin's record probably must stand as an all-time high—or low. Military carnage is usually short and quick, but Hardin's bloody activities spanned a period of approximately nine years.

As extraordinary as the record may be, even more extraordinary is the fact that, in an age of swift and summary justice, Wes Hardin, despite innumerable charges and indictments against him, was punished by the courts with only an assessed twenty-five-year penitentiary sentence, and a concurrent two-year stretch. Furthermore, the sentence was commuted, and after Hardin was released he was given a full pardon, with complete restoration of citizenship rights and privileges.

Many hardcover books have been written about him, and he appears in virtually all anthologies of western bad men. Yet, with the publication of his autobiography, it would have seemed likely that the mystery and glamour about him, if any, would have been removed. It remains the definitive book concerning the major part of his life.

THE LIFE
of
JOHN WESLEY HARDIN
from the
Original Manuscript
As Written by Himself

**Published by
Smith & Moore, Seguin, Texas
1896**

Price 50 Cents

This slender, crudely illustrated, 144-page volume of disintegrating paper is an oddity, and one that is alternately convincing and dubious.

In a preface, the publishers explain, "We are indebted to Hon. P.S. Sewell . . . for being able to publish this manuscript . . . with legal ability, he fought through the El Paso Courts, finally securing the manuscript for the heirs."

The book is not suspect beause it is fairly well written. John Wesley Hardin was the son of a preacher-teacher-lawyer, and was well educated for the times; eventually he became a practicing lawyer himself. But many of the statements and subsequent discrepancies provoke distrust in the cynical researcher. For example, when he writes:

"No, my readers, I have served twenty-five years for the killing of Webb but . . . there is a God in high heaven who knows that I did not shoot Charles Webb through malice or anger or for money, but to save my own life."

Hardin served only little more than half of twenty-five years, though it may have seemed like twenty-five years to him.

The average autobiographer cannot be expected to disclose all with the meticulous detail and vulgar elaboration of a Samuel Pepys. He will seek to delete or to minimize material that is unfavorable. Consequently, diaries and autobiographies are often interesting for what they patently conceal rather than for what they explicitly reveal.

We must assume that Hardin did write most or all of the Seguin booklet, since most of it deals with his murderous activities from the age of fifteen to the age of twenty-four; its details few people, if any, besides himself would know.

In the early part of it, he explains that the Civil War was raging when he was a boy of nine years, and that he tried to run away and fight the Yankees, after having seen Abraham Lincoln burned in effigy as "a demon who was waging a cruel and relentless war on the South, to rob her of her most sacred rights." So I grew up a rebel.

And therein, perhaps, lies an explanation of the phenomenon called John Wesley Hardin. Perhaps, though he came from what is popularly known as "good, solid American stock," he was a rare and unfortunate combination of genes and chromosomes which made him a rebel, a psychopath and an egoist, completely contemptuous of human life and wholly oblivious to any laws save those of his own desires.

However, as he related his version of the murders he committed, he invariably excused himself on grounds that he was either provoked or acting in defense of self or others, or acting for the good of the general public. There were also cases of justified and mandatory acts of revenge, he tells us, and, of course, several self-exonerations when he was "mistakenly" charged, being innocently elsewhere at the time.

Throughout the journal, he appears to himself to be a crusader with two missions in life. First, he was champion of "all good people against the crimes of brutal Negroes," especially those in the post-bellum police forces. Second, he was the unrelentng foe of mob rule and violence.

As for the first, the violence and misrule of venal appointed governors in the South is well-attested, and their renegade police force did include Negroes, who, in excess of new freedom, and from lack of experience, did kill and destroy more than they protected.

Hardin equally despised Mexicans and Indians and Yankees. His solution was over-simplified: it was to kill as many as he could and thoroughly intimidate the remainder.

As for the second point, it was quite true that with the breakdown of law and order, men of his day took the law into their own hands and attempted to protect or punish by mob, posse, or vigilante rule. Wes Hardin, however, was writing in retrospect. During his career, there was usually a price on his head and a very substantial price at that. He failed to record that the posses and mobs of which he disapproved were usually looking for him, and that consequently, he activated more mobs than he dispersed. Then too, his brother and cousins had been lynched by a mob which had gathered when Hardin murdered the officer whose death eventually resulted in his prison sentence.

He was a wanderer and remained nowhere long, except in the penitentiary where he had no option in the matter.

He visited and revisited a great many places and communities, some of which may still be well known, others which have vanished. One of the most unusual features of the autobiography is the revelation that the Hardin clan was an incredibly numerous one. Everywhere he went, there was an uncle or aunt or numerous cousins. Even an outlaw may have inlaws. There were relatively few inns or hotels, and, in the custom of the country, relatives who came visiting, however distant, dubious, or unexpected, were always received cordially and hospitably. Wes took frequent and extensive advantage of this pleasant custom.

John Wesley Hardin was born in Bonham, Texas, on May 26, 1853, the son of Reverend James Gibson Hardin, a Methodist preacher and circuit rider and his wife, Elizabeth, "a model wife and helpmate." There were several older children, but Reverend Hardin, hoping to dedicate this son to the ministry, fittingly bestowed on him the name of the founder of Methodism. John, or "Wes," almost immediately began to lend **credence** to the popular belief that the preacher's son is **always** the worst boy in town.

Evidently, the father was a firm believer in the theory that sparing the rod spoils the child, and Wes recounts many thrashings. Father Hardin, we are given to understand, used not a rod but a pliable rawhide.

As the Hardin family increased, the income from preaching became insufficient, especially since the pay was mostly in kind. Hardin's father was almost as peripatetic as his son turned out to be. He became a teacher, in addition to his preaching duties, and moved to and from various counties. He is said to have been at one time the pastor of a substantial and still active church in Dallas.

He also studied law, and was admitted to the bar in 1861, at length moving his family back to Trinity County, where he then preached, taught school and practiced law on the side.

It is worth observing that Wes mentions his mother appreciatively and briefly in the beginning of his book, but never thereafter. On the other hand, he nearly always came riding back to father to confess his crimes and to seek counsel, or sanctuary.

It was in Trinity County that he committed his first act of mayhem. He was only fourteen, and the incident was the result of an argument with Charles Sloter about a girl with the pleasantly nostalgic name of "Sal." Wes maintains that Sloter struck him first and drew a knife, whereupon Wes stabbed him twice, almost fatally, in the breast and back. Hardin claims that on learning the "facts," the school trustees exonerated him instead of expelling him, and that the courts rendered an acquittal verdict. "And," he adds with obvious relish, "I may mention that poor old Charley was long afterwards hung by a mob in an adjoining county." He failed to note the coincidence that it was for the murder of another man named Charles that he went to the penitentiary.

Before embarking on the story of his more mature years, which, by his reckoning began in 1868 when he was fifteen years old, he flings out this admonition: "Readers, you will see what drink and passion can do. If you wish to be successful in life, be temperate and control your passions. If you don't, ruin and death is the inevitable result." It was too bad that John Wesley Hardin had not reached these sage conclusions sooner. Within a year after he became fifteen, he had killed four men—all, of course, with justification.

The first murder took place when he went to visit an uncle, "carrying my pistol, of course." There, he and his cousin were matched in a wrestling bout with a huge Negro called "Mage," who over-estimated his prowess and agreed to take on the two boys at the same time. Mage lost the first fall quickly, and in suffering the second, had his face scratched by Wes, so that it bled copiously. Enraged by this, he threatened to kill Wes, but Uncle Barett interfered and discharged Mage.

According to Wes, the following day, returning home by horseback (he explains that he had gone eight or nine miles out of the way in order to "deliver a message"), he encountered Mage on a country road. The Negro, carrying a big stick, cursed him and grabbed the bridle of his horse, and tried to attack him. Wes produced his trusty Colt .44 and shot him "again and again." He then supposedly reported what he had done to still another uncle, who returned with him to the scene. Mage was still alive and cursing. Wes wanted to shoot him again, but his uncle restrained him, gave him a $20 gold piece, and told him to go home and explain everything to his father.

Mage died.

Father and Mother Hardin were sympathetic and distracted. Wes then proceeds to draw his picture of contemporary justice.

54

"All the courts were conducted by bureau agents and renegades who were inveterate enemies of the South, with a code which invariably ended in gross injustice to the Southern people. To be tried for killing a Negro meant certain death at the hands of a court, backed by Northern bayonets."

Wes's father had further explained to his son that justice and equity would never prevail again until there was restored to power the Democratic Party, which was then the party of moderation and conservatism. Under the circumstances, the only thing for Wes to do was to disappear until the time that law and order and, presumably, the Democratic Party, were restored.

His hideway at "old man Morgan's," was arranged by his brother, Joe, who was teaching school at a place called Logallis Prairie. Wes spent his time there hunting and fishing until Joe warned him that a detachment of United States soldiers were coming after him.

"But," writes Wes, "I went after them, instead of they after me." He ambushed them in a creek bed, killed the two white soldiers and put the third, a Negro, to flight. Overtaking him, he demanded surrender, "in the name of the Southern Confederacy." When the black man tried to shoot him, Wes gave him a bullet from the Colt .44.

"I waylaid them, as I had no mercy on men whom I know only wanted to get my body and torture and kill it."

The soldiers were buried in the creek bed, all their effects were burned, and obliging neighbors took permanent custody of their horses.

"And thus it was," he proclaims proudly, "that by the fall of 1868 I had killed four men and was myself wounded in the arm."

John Wesley Hardin had become a man, in a manner of speaking. He was fifteen years old and was by then current standards, an adult. He was a fine horseman, either for quick or long riding, as were all active men of his period. It was said he could gallop at full speed toward a tree to which a small target was tied, and draw and empty his pistol into the target's center without slackening his horse's speed.

Throughout his journal, he mentions "his good friend, the sheriff" of this or that county, and there is no reason to believe he exaggerates. Law men too lived by the gun, and held respect for a fast draw. Frequently he was protected and assisted by lawmen. The rewards for John Wesley Hardin were offered by the State, and the last thing some county sheriffs wanted was to cooperate with a carpetbagger state government.

Wes, like all other outlaws, was no lone wolf. His companions were usually cousins or other relatives, sometimes almost a gang of them, and the personnel changed frequently. Except for gambling, he was sharp in money matters; he was never accused of theft, though he was frequently a victim. He was a compulsive gambler and nearly always won, sometimes large sums. He admits, however, that he had "a method," which required cooperation of his partner, who played or stood close by. Wes was a hard loser and always attributed his loss to someone else's cheating.

He was reported to be successful in business; dealing and speculating in cattle, hides, horses, and other fast-moving commodities. He made a considerable amount of money, but it always slipped rapidly through his fingers.

In January, 1869, still fifteen, we find Wes engaged with his father in teaching school at Pisga, in Navarro County. He proudly relates that his class consisted of "twenty-five scholars, both girls and boys, from the age of 6 to 16 years." What a school it must have been, and what a teacher! A school term lasted then the three winter months, as children had to help plant crops in spring, cultivate in summer, and harvest them in the fall. Wes was offered a renewal for the next year, but, he "had conceived the idea of becoming a cowboy, and as my cousins were in the business, we began to drive cattle to shipping points. Of course, in this kind of life I soon learned to play poker, seven-up, and euchre, and it was only a short time until I would banter for the best for a game."

Actually, his dexterity in shuffling and dealing cards rivalled his expertise with a gun. He also liked fast horses, and would bet on anything from a horse race to "spitting at a crack."

Before the autumn of 1869, when his brother Joe came to see him and persuaded him to come back with him to Hill County, a few minor incidents occurred. In writing his book, Wes did not have the power of total recall. He admits he had forgotten having shot a man's left eye out "on a bet" until a friend some years afterward reminded him of losing a bottle of whiskey to him on the wager. He did clearly remember that a detachment of Yankees came to capture him and failed. Even more vividly he recalled that he had a cousin named "Simp" Dixon, nineteen years old, "who belonged to the 'Ku Kluck Klan', and was sworn to kill Yankee soldiers." "His (Simp's) mother, brother and sister, were tortured and killed by United States soldiers because of their loyalty to the Southern cause." There was a big reward for Cousin Simp, and Wes "sympathized with him in every way and was generally with him." A squad of soldiers came upon them in the Richland bottom. "When the battle was over, two soldiers lay dead. Simp killed one and I the other, while the rest escaped."

In any event, in the fall of 1869, Joe and Wes Hardin, travelling to Hill County, stopped briefly in Hillsboro, Texas with "Aunt Anne," and then moved out into the country with an uncle. It must have been dull, and Wes rode on to Brazos, where he speculated in cotton and hides, played cards, and bet on the races. He formed a partnership with a man named Joe Collins (who had married a cousin), and "things ran smoothly for some time . . . we were doing well until a tragedy occurred that forever dissolved our partnership."

Wes's father had come to visit him on a typical paternal mission, importuning him to come home and live a life of rectitude. He borrowed his father's horse on Christmas Eve and rode off to the races with Collins, where they won a pot of money and adjourned to the saloon poker game. Collins did not play, but he was there, ostensibly as a spectator, and "the method" was working. The losers, headed by Jim Bradley, "a bully and leader of the local gang," were dissatisfied, and reversed the results by taking all the money and Wes's boots and gun, to boot. When Wes was properly outfitted again, he shot Bradley with a Remington .45. Bradley's gang then got into action.

"I soon found the situation was critical," Wes admits. "The whole country, except for a few relatives and friends, had turned out to hunt me; in fact, there was a regular mob after me whose avowed purpose was to hang me." He managed to reach his father at two in the morning, and although his father was disappointed that Wes would not be riding home with him, they agreed that the next best thing for Wes was to try and make it back there by way of the opposite side of the river. However, circumstances made that inadvisable, so Wes rode off toward Brenham with Aleck Barrickman to visit "Uncle Bob." At Nob Hill, the first stop, they found a travelling circus in town. All the beds at the inn were filled. It was a cold night and they joined the circus roustabouts at their campfire. Wes "accidentally" struck the hand of a circus man who was lighting his pipe with a fagot, and although apologies were profuse, an argument resulted.

"He started to pull his gun," Wes records, "I pulled mine and fired. He fell with a .45 ball through his head. Barrickman covered the crowd . . . until I could saddle our horses and we rode off, apparently to the north and then changed our course south."

Next stop, Kosse. Wes precedes the brief episode with a confession: "I was young then and loved every pretty girl I met, and at Kosse I met one and we got along together famously. I made an engagement to call on her that night and did so." Apparently Wes was a victim of the old badger game, but he doesn't seem to have realized it. At the appropriate moment, the outraged paramour of the girl burst in the door and finding them **in flagrante delictu**, demanded financial reparation.

In handing over his money, Wes intentionally dropped some of it on the floor. As the conspirator was bent over retrieving it, Wes let him have it "between the eyes."

At Uncle Bob's, he farmed for a while, but when it became known that the state police were being reorganized and strengthened, Wes considered it prudent to move on. He wandered from place to place visiting relatives and, at length, got back to father, only to have his brother, Joe, write and ask him to come down to Round Rock and graduate with him from Professor Landrum's school. Wes went, and passed the diploma examinations in one day.

"But," he writes, "the rewards that were being offered for me made that country too dangerous a place for me to stop." He resolved to go to Shreveport, Louisiana, to visit—what else—relatives.

At Longview, Texas, he was arrested by mistake, for a charge of which he was innocent, but one of the officers thought Wes resembled or was a man wanted for a crime committed in Waco, Texas. Wes, for a change, was blameless. Three officers started across the country with him, but when two of them went into a town to buy supplies, Wes killed the other, stole his horse, and rode home again to father at Mount Calm.

Mount Calm belied its name. His father sent the stolen horse back—a point of honor—and concluded that the only safe place for his errant son was Mexico. Accordingly, Wes set forth, but near Belton, Texas, was arrested again, "by men calling themselves police." The arresting officers had several bottles of whiskey with them and made the mistake of indulging themselves too freely. With their caution dulled, Wes shot three of them and made it back to father and friends, "to tell them all good-bye once more."

This time his father decided there would be no slip-up, and rode as far as Belton with his son. But when Wes came to Austin, he could not resist making a detour and stopping at Gonzales to visit more relatives. He found them gathering cattle for a drive to Abilene, Kansas, and when they urged Wes to join them, assuring him he would be perfectly safe from arrest, well-paid, and have a wonderful time, he decided to go.

During the intervening wait, he visited a Mexican encampment nearby, killed one Mexican in a crooked monte game, injured several others, and caused so many injuries in general that the frightened Mexicans moved away. And he met a girl named Jane Bowen, with whom he fell deeply and permanently in love.

In March, 1871, now seventeen, Wes started up the Chisolm trail to Kansas. In performing his duties on the trail, he was able to maintain his average by killing five Mexican cattle drivers and two Indians. One of the Indians was shot, we are told, just as he was detected in the act of letting go an arrow directed at Wes.

For allowing the cattle to pass through the Osage Nation, the Indians levied a transit tax, usually of cattle, since the white man had decimated the buffalo herds from which the Indians had lived. A mounted Osage brave attempted to cut out one of Wes's steers.

"He was armed and drew, saying that if I did not let him cut the beef out he would kill the animal. I told him that if he killed the animal I would kill him. Well, he killed the beef and I killed him."

He mounted the dead Indian on the dead steer as a grim warning, to whomever might be concerned.

In Abilene, Kansas, where he arrived June 1, and which

he described as the worst of all fast towns he had ever seen, he drew his pay and met and socialized with some of his notorious colleagues, including Wild Bill Hickok.

He also, reputedly, eliminated some of his lesser rivals who were pushing up uncomfortably from below, and gambled and raised hell in general.

Wes Hardin had no sense of humor and he seems to have realized it at times. In his matter-of-fact narrative, he relates an instance of burglary while sleeping in his hotel room. He shot the intruder but somehow, in the resulting confusion, he lost his pistols and pants. When the mob came after him, as it always did, he jumped out a second-story window in his "night clothes"—by which he meant his long drawers. He burrowed in a haystack which "he knew about." The mob debated burning the haystack on the theory he was concealed there, but did not because of its proximity to a building. When the mob departed, Wes crawled out the other side, stole a horse, and professes to have been hilarious at the memory of galloping madly across country to his friend's camp, clad only in "night clothes."

The story is unconvincing.

In fact, readers having come that far in the biography must have felt a curious sort of disappointment throughout. At no place has he mentioned the wonders and beauties of the wild and magnificent country in which he spent his life. There were for Hardin no stars or moonlight, no sunshine or shadow, no colors or perfumes, no warmth, no conversation around camp fires.

He never mentions what anyone looked like, except "a hoary-haired old man," "a pretty girl at Kosse" and his wife, "the prettiest girl in the world." He either did not observe or didn't care to record what people wore, what sort of houses they lived in, or what they ate. Apparently he drank only whiskey—a great deal of it—and mentioned only his first prison breakfast and the "dainty dishes" prepared for him by the wife of one of his captors. He did hear the howling wolves near the Chisolm Trail, those hungry creatures that had formerly fed on buffalo herds and now were attracted by the scent of cattle. He did not hear the rain. He did not feel the heat of the sun or the cool south breeze, and he did not hear the crash of thunder or see the flash of lightning, except for that produced by gun or pistol. He did refer a few times to a cold, frosty night, and once of having walked in the snow at prison. He mentions The Diety more in expletive than in awe or worship, but he may have had enough of that when young and at home.

Wes Hardin was simply a wild young animal with a thin veneer of civilization. Like the animal, he accepted life in all its moods and manifestations, without wonder, without remembrance of the past or anticipation of any more than the immediate future, except solely as related to his own survival and pleasure. He wrote his journal in the stark, unadorned manner, except to insist on his high-minded crusading spirit and to belabor his justification.

Wes Hardin got back to Uncle Barnett's, in Hill County, on July 30, 1871, and resumed his fight against scalawag governor E.J. Davis and his infamous police of "crooks and ignorant Negroes." In one of their raids, three of these police came across Wes in a grocery store. He killed two of them. Other Negroes in the county and those in adjoining counties organized a posse of protest and revolt, threatening to depopulate the whites. Wes got twenty-five men together and warned the blacks that if they tried to carry out their threat, there would not be enough of them left to tell the tale. This took care of the local situation, we are told, and when a Negro mob came from Austin to get him, he supposedly killed three of them and sent the rest running for home.

Then he writes, "Nothing of importance happened until I married Jane Bowen, although we were expecting the police at any time."

To him, she was the "prettiest and sweetest girl in the

world." She could not have realized the extent of the trials and tribulations she was letting herself in for. But once committed, she never wavered. Marriage did not change Wes very much; he was away from home most of the time and despite this—or perhaps because of it—their love continued until her death.

On June 5, 1872, Wes took "a bunch of horses to East Texas" to sell. "Nothing unusual happened on the trip," he records, "except at Willis some fellows tried to arrest me for carrying a pistol, but they got the contents thereof instead."

And on return, he likewise enters, "Nothing unusual happened until I got to Polk County." There at Gates Saloon and Ten Pin Alley, he got into a dispute over a bowling game. The loser insulted him and fired one barrel of a shotgun at him and missed. Wes "did not want to get into any new trouble" and merely returned a harmless "courtesy shot." But the lowdown loser discharged the other barrel and ran. Wes was hit and collapsed.

Cousin Barnett Jones, who happened to be along, took custody of the money belt holding some $2500 in gold and silver, and carried Wes to a doctor's office. It was decided by the doctor, and a colleague whom he called in for consultation, that "Wes had had it."

"Ordinarily speaking," Wes comments, "the wounds were fatal, but there was a chance, if I would be submissive; and they thought they could save me if I could stand an operation without opiates. If I died, I wanted my head clear. So they went to work with knives and forceps." Two buckshot had ploughed through his right kidney and lodged between spine and ribs; two others hit his silver belt buckle, which saved his life. "Everybody thought I would die, but I told friends to cut the wires to Austin so they could not send papers for me."

He was put in the hotel, where he received excellent attention, but on August 15, he was told he had to move or risk being arrested. He was still bed-ridden at this point, but doctors agreed he might be carried to a private home, which he was, and then he was moved again, by hack, to the doctor's house at Sumpter.

"Everybody tried to help," he explains, "but as usual the infamous police were after me along with the mischief-makers."

He had to be moved several times—unable to stand or walk—and, finally, went back to the doctor's home again.

On August 27 he had to move in a hurry, but by that time was able to mount a horse, assisted by the doctor's son, Billy, and he rode to the home of his friend named Harrell, in Angelina County. On September 1, (1872), he received word that two policemen were on their way there to get him. Only Mrs. Harrell was at home with Wes when they arrived. The policemen insulted the uncooperative woman. Wes, reclining on a pallet, shot and killed both of them, but not before one had shot him in the thigh. He claims that at the inquest of these murders, the verdict was "death at the hands of an unknown party."

In his own words, he was "in a bad fix now" with a new wound and the others not healed. He rode to the home of another friend and sent word to Sheriff Dick Reagan of Cherokee County that he would make a deal; the conditions being that Wes would surrender, provided he was given protection from mob violence, medical aid and half the rewards offered for him. The sheriff agreed and arrived on September 4th, but in the excitement of seeing the notorious Hardin, the deputy grew over-zealous and shot Wes in the knee. The sheriff was embarrassed and apologetic.

"The Sheriff and others were all very sorry that this happened," and each seemed to "vie with each other in making me as comfortable as possible. They got a hack and put pillows and bed quilts on it, trying to make my journey easy." He lodged first at a private house in Rusk, was given medical attention, and subsequently was moved to the hotel. The sheriff's son became his nurse, and the sheriff's wife outdid herself in cooking for him.

He hoped he might be cleared of several capital crimes charged against him on Gonzales. After a stop at a hotel in Austin, and then the Austin jail, he arrived in shackles at Gonzales where the citizens, seeing their "hero and champion" so humiliated and degraded, "denounced it." Sheriff Jones had the irons cut off and put Wes in jail. But wooden walls did not a prison make, and on October 10, 1872, he sawed his way out, assisted by an admiring guard who masked the sound of sawing with other noises.

Wes was nineteen.

He went home to his "darling and beloved wife," and then was seen at Cuero, some twenty-five miles from his home, where he engaged in cattle shipping.

At a card game in Cuero, where he was the big winner, a tipsy admirer named J.B. Morgan suggested that Wes buy him a bottle of champagne. When Wes refused, Morgan became obnoxious. He left and then returned, stating he had been insulted and asking Wes if he were armed. Wes was. Morgan reached for his gun but before he got it halfway out, Wes shot him through the left eye, killing him.

(This may have been the incident, misplaced in time and location, about which his friend reminded him later.)

Wes went to the stable, got his horse and rode away unmolested. It was for this murder he later received a concurrent two year penitentiary sentence for manslaughter.

The most tragic event was yet to come. Previously, his brother, Joe, had moved to Comanche, Texas, and on a visit to him, Wes left his favorite race horse, "Hondo," in Joe's charge. In the latter part of April, 1874, Wes returned to Comanche to train "Hondo" for the upcoming races to be held there on May 26th. By the time of the race, his wife, his parents and various other relatives had arrived. His brother and his cousin, Bud Dixon, also had entries in the race. This event, widely advertised, happened to be held on the day of Hardin's birthday.

There is no indication that the race was fixed, but by sheer luck, no doubt, Wes's "Hondo" came in first, Joe's "Shiloh" placed second, and Bud's "Dock" came in third. Wes won $3000 in cash, fifty head of cattle, fifteen horses, and several wagons.

After the races, it was customary for all to meet at the saloon for a celebration of the winners and, on this occasion, of Wes Hardin's birthday.

Sometime earlier, Wes had been informed that a deputy sheriff named Charles Webb, had come to Comanche County from Brown County for the purpose of capturing Jim Taylor, who was a friend of Wes', and perhaps also for the purpose of killing Wes Hardin. Webb had no authority outside Brown County, except in "hot pursuit" of a fleeing criminal, so if he planned to kill Wes Hardin, it would be in the role of a despicable bounty hunter. There were large rewards for Hardin, however, and with him dead, no one would be likely to interpose technicalities.

Wes had seen Webb at the races, but they had had no contact there. After a few hours of merrymaking at the saloon, brother Jefferson Davis, also a member of the family group, wanted to take Wes home, and Wes agreed to go. As he was leaving the saloon, Charles Webb, wearing two six-shooters, entered. Wes invited him to a traditional cigar and drink, but Webb drew a pistol and shot Wes "the length of his left side." Although wounded, Wes's answering shot caught Webb in the left check, killing him. There was more shooting and a crowd quickly gathered.

The county sheriff, John Karnes, ("my friend," Wes writes) came on the scene and asked for particulars. Wes admitted killing Webb in self-defense and handed his pistol to the sheriff. He asked protection from the mob which was assembling. But this time, Wes was to really meet a mob and he was unarmed. The sheriff was overpowered, and friends and relatives found the odds too great. Wes managed to escape but his relatives were not so fortunate. On June 5, at midnight, a mob of one-hundred fifty men took Joe Hardin, Bud Dixon and Dixon's brother Tom, bareheaded and barefoot, through the streets to the postoaks at the edge of town and hanged them. The next day, two more of Wes Hardin's friends were killed the same way.

Wes made it back to Gonzales with difficulty, and in pain, and settled up all his "cow debts," went to Brenham after his "loving wife," and prepared to depart. "I was now about to leave," he explains sadly, "not because I was an outlaw but because mob law had become supreme in Texas, as the hanging of my relatives and friends proved."

He travelled overland with a friend to New Orleans where, by prearrangement, he met his wife and child, who had been accompanied that far by Harry Swain, the town marshall of Brenham. (Swain had married a Hardin cousin.)

Out of appreciation to Swain apparently, Hardin became "J.W. Swain." He and his wife and child took a steamboat to Cedar Keys, Florida, and at Gainesville, Florida, Wes bought a saloon. On the first day it was opened, two old friends recognized him but promised to keep quiet. On the third day, he killed a Negro, presumably one of a mob which was protesting the arrest of a Negro. In any case, after this Wes sold out and moved to Miconopy, where he set up another bar, horse-traded, and contracted to supply beef to butchers. When they reneged, he went into the butcher business himself, along with the liquor business, and found both highly profitable.

Meanwhile, gambling remained his first love and most remunerative operation.

He was doing well and was happy until the middle of April when, he relates, "Two Pinkerton detectives came to Florida and found me out." But the Sheriff and Marshall were his friends, he said and "put me on to the Pinkertons.

I at once concluded to leave Jacksonville with a policeman named Gus Kennedy. We were going to New Orleans, intending to go to old Mexico, but the Pinkertons followed and came upon us near the Florida-Georgia border. A fight was the natural result."

Wes and Gus each killed a Pinkerton detective. The names of the victims are obscured in the mists of time, but when Hardin killed his, a bell rang somewhere. He had killed forty men. His record would stand at that figure.

He and Gus Kennedy continued the journey, arriving at Mobile, Alabama, where, as pre-arranged, Mrs. J.H. Swain and children (there were two now, Molly and John W.,) were registered already at the hotel. Wes and Gus proceeded to a poker game where they won $3500, and then Wes travelled to Polland where he stayed with his wife's uncle. Wes, in that section of the country, had run out of relatives, but his wife had a few, and in due time, he gathered another coterie of kindred souls, all birds of a feather. He invested in the logging business with Shop Hardie, and the results were profitable.

Texas was among the last of the states to be readmitted to the union. Governor Hubbard was the legally elected governor, and there had been a complete reorganization and activation of the state police known as The Texas Rangers. They ranged far to get John Wesley Hardin. A young captain named Armstrong determined to bring Hardin in and he drafted Ranger Jack Duncan, a specialist deputy. After conferring with Governor Hubbard, and arranging for speedy extradition process, they set out for Polland.

Wes explained that they resorted to highly unethical practices in order to locate him, such as tampering with and opening United States mails.

In any case, as Wes tells it, "partner and self concluded to go to Pensacola to buy supplies and, of course, to play cards. We all soon got into a poker game, Shipley and I having a system understood between us which proved a winner." (Shipley was general manager of the railroad, completely untrustworthy and disloyal, and he knew that J.W. Swain was, in fact, J.W. Hardin. Despite his handsome winnings in the poker game, he advised the Rangers of the return travel plans, including a stopover in Pensacola.)

The Rangers had twenty men concealed around the hotel where Wes was staying. The train had to be made up at the junction, and the baggage and smoking cars were set out on a siding alongside the hotel. Wes and his five travelling companions decided to start a poker game in the smoking car, awaiting makeup and departure of the train. It was a simple matter for the Rangers to surprise and capture him, although one of Wes's friends was killed in the melee. The train pulled out on time with Wes Hardin as prisoner.

He tried to get released by writ of **habeas corpus** but the case was postponed and the extradition papers arrived before the case was heard. He was taken by train to Texas. At every station, curious crowds had gathered, anxious to see the famous outlaw, but he was kept in strict seclusion.

Before they reached Austin, warning came that a tremendous number of people had gathered at the railroad station. Both Wes and his guards were afraid it might mean mob violence. The train was stopped before it reached the station and Wes was rushed to the jail in a hack.

He stayed in the Austin jail until the latter part of September when the entire troop of Company 35 of the Texas Rangers, accompanied by Sheriff Wilson and deputies, "escorted" him to Comanche. The town was 160 miles from Austin and the trip took several days.

"Our military appearance created interest in every town," he wrote with pride. "I rode in a buggy with Sheriff Wilson, preceded by the Ranger Company, and the other escort bringing up the rear. We camped out every night and the escort was very considerate except that I was chained."

On arrival at Comanche, he had to be carried into the jail because the chains were heavy for him to walk with them. Hardin explained that the reason for such a strong guard was fear of "the brutal mob," the fear that the mob which had hung his relatives would hang him, and in fact, a mob of several hundred was camped outside town with the stated intention of administering justice in case the court failed to do so. The Ranger Captain, sensing the tension and violent feeling, deputized an additional thirty-five citizens to help protect Wes. And then the Captain announced that if there were an attack on the jail, he would arm Wes Hardin and let him "rough it out." This statement, Hardin would have us believe, aroused sufficient fear to completely evaporate the possibility of mob violence.

Wes Hardin complained bitterly of the injustice of his trial and, for once, he complained with some justification. He had two lawyers and, on the face of it, they did not put up a very good defense. They permitted his record to be put in evidence and apparently he was tried as much on it as for the crime specified in his indictment. Only three years before, his "own brothers and cousins had met death at the hands of a mob here," in the town where he was being tried, and clearly, there should have been a change of venue. He even claimed that six of the jurors had been members of the mob which had hung his relatives, and that the judge was prejudiced, having advised others in connection with the case. He did not have one single witness who could testify that he acted in self-defense. "All had either been lynched or driven out of the country." Even the state admitted that Charles Webb had fired at Hardin twice and wounded him once before Hardin drew his pistol and killed him.

Nevertheless, John Wesley Hardin was found guilty of murder in the second degree, and his punishment assessed at twenty-five years imprisonment. The case was appealed; he was taken back to Austin during the pendency of appeal; the decision was affirmed, and Wes was returned to Comanche to be sentenced.

Then began one of the most extraordinary spectacles in the history of gunmen and outlaws. Everyone with the slightest conception of law and justice realized that Hardin, outlaw and murderer though he was, had not received a fair or impartial trial at Comanche, and there was a great change in public sentiment to his favor.

The procession started out from Comanche bound for Huntsville Penitentiary with "four prisoners chained by twos in a wagon and guarded by a sheriff and a company of Rangers." It was the same escort and formation which took Wes to Comanche and had excited so much attention.

"Of course great crowds would flock from everywhere to see the notorious John Wesley Hardin from hoary-headed farmers to little maids in their teens." It was one of the latter who exclaimed that he was "so handsome," and to whom he replied, with modest disparagement, that his wife thought so.

The nearest railroad point was Fort Worth. He writes, "When we got to Fort Worth, the people turned out like a Fourth of July picnic and I had to get out of the wagon and shake hands for an hour before my guard could get me through the crowd. We arrived there on October 1, 1878 and stopped in Fort Worth all day and night . . . People everywhere pressed 20, 50 and 100 dollar gold pieces in my hand and crowds would come all along the route to see us, especially at Palestine. I was astonished to see even the convicts in stripes gazing at me when we got inside the walls of the penitentiary."

On arrival at the prison he was given a hearty breakfast, consisting of coffee, bacon, bread and molasses. His hair was cut and he was shaved, stripped, bathed, and his body minutely examined for scars and marks. He was twenty-five years old. He weighed 165 pounds, was five feet ten inches tall, had curling brown hair and gray eyes, and he became prisoner No. 7109. Photographs of him, like all those of the period, show him with the usual glum and wooden expression, and he would not be remembered as either particularly comely or ill-favored.

In a comparatively recent Hardin biography, a sympathetic biographer blandly indicates that Hardin was a good man in prison, that prison officials expressed pride in him. He intimates further that Hardin received commutation of his sentence for exemplary conduct, eventually receiving a full pardon. This is somewhat at variance with his prison records, which shows the following punitive items:

January 1879 . . . . 39 lashes for mutinous conduct
January 1880 . . . . 20 lashes for conspiracy to escape
May 1881 . . . . solitary confinement in dark cell
February 1883 . . . . solitary confinement in dark cell
July 1883 . . . . punishment for disorder
October 1893 . . . . punishment for laziness, three cases
June 1893 . . . . 20 lashes for inciting to riot

The last listing is only a year before his release. It is possible his conduct was good for the time preceding his discharge.

He was first assigned to the wheelwright's shop. He promptly organized or joined a plot with seventy-five other convicts to tunnel underground, through five brick walls, to the armory where guns and ammunition were kept. No explanation is made of how the excavated dirt and material, which had to be considerable, was disposed of. When the tunnel was completed, except for the final breakthrough of a wooden floor, traitors hoping for reward of special privileges gave the show away, and Wes, with nine other prisoners was put in irons and confined to a dark cell for fifteen days, on bread and water. By "irons" were meant a ball and chain in addition to shackles.

When he was returned to duty, he was put to work in the factory. Here he manufactured a bolt, he said, which enabled him to free himself at will from his ball and chain, and then he artfully manufactured keys for the padlocks to twenty cells, as well as for the outer gates. Again a traitorous cellmate tipped off the guards. Wes complained, "All my associates were Judases and Benedict Arnolds."

For the key-making activity, he received a flogging which he describes in brutal detail.

The offender was stripped, his hands and feet were loosely tied together, and he was put belly-downward in spread-eagle fashion on the floor, with two men holding arms and legs taut by ropes extending from them. The underkeeper then took a strip 20 inches long and 2 and one-fourth inches thick, attached to a handle 12 inches long, and "he began to whip my naked body with this instrument. They were now flogging me and every lick left the imprint of every lash of which there were four in this whip, consisting of thick pieces of harness leather."

An overseer stood by, calling out the number of strokes in measures, sepulchral tones. Sometimes the overseer lost count, although thirty-one strokes was considered maximum.

Wes remembers having heard "Don't hit him in the same place so often."

He recorded that his "sides and back were beaten into a jelly and while quivering and bleeding . . . forced to walk in the snow to another building where . . . was confined in a dark cell and threatened with death unless . . . revealed details of the plot." He remained there for four days.

It is obvious that jailers and wardens of the period placed no faith in the reformation or rehabilitation of hardened criminals. Today, attempts at escape by prisoners are not considered abnormal and are properly penalized by lighter and summary sentences. Wes claims that punishments he received were for offenses of which he was innocent or meaningless punishments meant as deterrents.

He wrote his wife that, though a prisoner, he was on the road to progress. He stated that he and a friend named "John" were members of a society and were "looked upon as leaders" by their associates, of which there were a "goodly number." Further, that friend "John," was president of the Moral and Christian Society, and that Wes, personally, was secretary of the Debating Club.

Faithful wife Jane wrote him complete reports of herself and the children. Although Hardin's journal is filled with egoistic concern, he never so much as mentions the birthplaces, dates or names of the children. Perhaps he hadn't been there when they were born, or perhaps he didn't remember. Jane is said to have written him more than a thousand letters during his confinement and he replied to these as he could, giving husbandly advice and fatherly counsel, and no material assistance.

He claims that he became a "constant reader" in the years from 1880 to 1882, and in the latter year had studied theology. The last paragraph of the Seguin publication reads:

"In 1885 I conceived the idea of studying law and wrote to the superintendent asking for his advice about what to read in order to have a practical knowledge of both civil and criminal law. He referred me to Col. A.T. McKinney of the Huntsville bar. In a few days I received the following:"

There follows a copy of the letter dated at Huntsville, May 6, 1889, addressed to Hon. Thos. Goree, listing recommended law texts and signed A.T. McKinney. Below this is the publisher's terse note:

"Here abruptly ends the Hardin manuscript."

But it was not by any means the end of John Wesley Hardin.

One closes the booklet with a mixture of disgust and relief. It has been little more than an account of wholesale murder. The writer would have one believe that his inclination to violence resulted from his having been a product of the terrible years which followed the War Between the States. But he was no more so than the average boy.

Only a perceptive psychiatrist could co-relate Wes Hardin, boy and man. In the autobiography, there is no recounting of happy recollections of childhood, but there are emphasized the frequent beatings received from his father, and he describes those with a sort of joy-in-penance.

Never having had a normal boyhood, he never grew into mature manhood. After each of his subsequent crimes, he ran straight-away to his father to report his derelictions and to be shriven by confession, just as when younger he had made expiation by taking a whipping.

Freud and Jung had not begun to delve into the mysteries of the mind, but Wes Hardin's confessions, though not made from the comfort of a couch, would have provided interesting material for clinical study. He was a psychotic killer and his murders followed the same familiar pattern. He was intelligent and he fully realized that in the penitentiary, where he was under constant guard and surveillance, his transgressions would be discovered. It is convincingly clear that he took his punishments with masochistic pleasure; he wrote of his floggings in lingering detail.

Wes Hardin longed to breathe the outside air and to see his wife and children. In studying law, he hit upon a clever scheme. He had been indicted at Cuero for killing J.B. Morgan, for whom he had declined to buy a bottle of champagne. It occurred to him that if he pled guilty and was taken there for sentencing, he would have an opportunity to see his family living nearby. With this in mind, he wrote to Mr. W.S. Fly, an able and highly respected attorney, with whom he had been acquainted at Cuero. He explained his hope and outlined his plan. Attorney Fly, in admiration of Hardin's cleverness, and with the typical do-gooder's belief that silk purses may be made from sow's ears, made the arrangements. The District Attorney, no doubt delighted to get the old case off his docket, was agreeable to accepting a plea of guilty to manslaughter, and to recommend a two-year sentence, to run concurrently with that already imposed.

There was a dramatic and happy family reunion at Cuero, and, although plans for a commutation application by Mr. Fly may have been started at that time, Wes had to go back to Huntsville Penitentiary.

A few months later, came the heavy blow: on November 6, 1892, Jane Bowen Hardin, worn by work and weary of waiting, died. At one place in his biography he wrote "she was as true as the magnet to the steel." It was not an especially good metaphor and it was inverted. The true steel was in Jane Bowen Hardin. She had fed, clothed and decently raised her children by sewing and washing, and selling milk, butter, chickens and eggs.

Two years after this, Wes was released from Huntsville Penitentiary. He had served nearly fifteen years and was forty-one years old. Pardoned but penniless, he went immediately to Gonzales to live with his children. He received a great many letters of congratulations and good wishes. Most important of all was one from his friend Attorney Fly, now Associate Justice of the Court of Appeals:

> "Enclosed herewith I send a full pardon from the Governor of Texas and I congratulate you on its reception and trust it is the dawn of a bright and peaceful future."

It was a letter of transmittal, with a full pardon by Governor J.S. Hogg, with restoration to full citizenship with right of suffrage.

The letter contained many of the usual cliches and

grandiloquent phrases common to the legal profession of the time: "There is time to retrieve a lost past . . . fix your eyes on the future . . . the hand of every man will be extended to help you . . . I trust the name of Hardin in the future will be associated with the performance of deeds that will ennoble his family and be a blessing to humanity." It ended with a recommendation that he read Victor Hugo's **Les Miserables,** the fictitious story of a man's self-redemption.

John Wesley Hardin was now ready to begin his new life as a practicing attorney. Then as now, a large percentage of public office-seekers were lawyers by profession, and while Wes was not so foolish as to actually become a political candidate, he became very active in the race for sheriff. So active, in a race that got so hot, that when his candidate lost, he found it advisable to move to Karnes County. Brother Jefferson Davis was living at Junction, Texas and he wrote Wes that there was a wonderful opening there for a good lawyer.

So Wes, confident of his ability, went to West Texas to live, and there romance came again, but briefly.

While on a visit to the usually convenient cousins in the vicinity of Junction, he met a very pretty girl named Callie Lewis. Callie was the daughter of a prominent and prosperous rancher and, although she was younger than Wes Hardin's own daughter, he fell in love with her. Her parents, oddly enough in view of the disparity of ages and the shady reputation of the suitor, were favorably, and even enthusiastically, inclined. Callie was presumably both flattered and flustered from the ardent wooing of so famous a beau, but she was coy and reluctant. At last, however, she accepted his proposal and early one afternoon, they were married in Junction.

Happy friends immediately set about arranging a rip-roaring supper and ball to celebrate the occasion. Jeff Davis Hardin took the couple to the home of a friend, there to enjoy a few honeymoon hours before the festivities began. On leaving them, he chided John Wesley for having "robbed the cradle."

At last, the preparations were completed, and the happy guests, including the bride's parents, assembled. They waited . . . and waited. But the bride and groom never arrived. The parents of the bride slipped out, and found the bride and groom still at the friend's house. Callie was hysterical, and sobbing violently. In the interval, we must suppose she had had enough of impetuous Wes, perhaps too much. At any rate, the distressed parents sorrowfully led her home and while there were never any explanations, Mr. and Mrs. Lewis made it plain that their sympathy was with the groom.

Wes may have felt some embarrassment and chagrin, but there were none so reckless as to inquire or joke. In any case, Junction was too quiet a town, and when he received word from a friend named Miller that a defense lawyer was needed at Pecos, he moved on. We are told he spent this period working on his memoirs. Here, again, the mystery of this composition becomes bothersome. As noted before, the last entry was a letter dated May 6, 1889. He was pardoned in 1894 and he married Callie Lewis in January, 1895. It does not seem consistent with man or plan for him to publish his book without at least his triumphal vindication in the commuted sentence and full pardon by the Governor of the State of Texas.

He did not tarry long at Pecos. It was inevitable that he should move on to El Paso, a big, bawdy, frontier city, a combination of Sodom and Gomorrah, filled with bad places and bad people, plain or fancy. No sensible or well-dressed man there would venture on the streets after nightfall without wearing a gun or two. The principal difference between gunmen and lawmen was that the latter wore badges.

John Wesley Hardin's reputation served him well in El Paso; he was among people who knew of it and appreciated it; and he promptly became one of the most sought-after criminal lawyers in town.

He gave his clients all the time he had left after his steady gambling and heavy drinking.

One fine day, an overly plump, highly painted, golden-blondine "living doll," walked into his law office. She was Mrs. Martin McRose, and indeed, McRose was a rose, fulsome and fullblown, with no visible thorns. She had, she said, a problem, and was seeking legal counsel, as well as sympathy and consolation. Her husband was in jail at Juarez, the Mexican counterpart to El Paso across the Rio Grande. Mr. McRose was involved with several criminal groups, one of which wanted him extradited to El Paso, and another wanting him to stay where he was. This was in April, the early part of the month, and in the land of mañana, the affair dragged along interminably, until Mr. McRose was shot while attempting to escape from jail.

Mrs. McRose sought more consolation in the arms of her lawyer where, perhaps, she had already found a great deal. She soon became known as "Wes Hardin's Woman," or "Hardin's McRose."

On an occasion when Wes was out of town, McRose got riotously drunk and appeared on the streets in disarray; shouting, brandishing and shooting a pistol, and otherwise disturbing the peace of the city. Encountering her, young Policeman John Selman Jr., instead of exercising a dignified restraint, hauled her off to the calaboose where she was fined fifty dollars. When Wes returned and learned about it, he was furious. But he did nothing about it immediately. In fact, it was several weeks before he met Selman's father, Constable John Selman Sr., and then it was a chance meeting on the street.

We'll let Selman Sr. tell what happened:

"I met Wes Hardin at 7 o'clock last evening close to the Acme saloon. When we met, Hardin said: 'you've got a son that is a bastardly, cowardly son of a bitch.'

I said 'Which one?'

The foregoing is quoted precisely from Selman's statement as it appeared in the **El Paso Daily Herald** of August 20, 1895. It continues:

"Hardin said: 'John, the one that is on the police force. He pulled my woman when I was absent and robbed her of $50, which they would not have done if I had been there.' I said: 'Hardin, there is no man on earth that can talk about my children like that without fighting, you cowardly son of a bitch.' "

Calling a man a bastard or a son of a bitch was the vilest possible insult, and required retaliation. This was before usage had given uneasy sanction to such terms. The newspaper interview with Constable Selman continues:

"Hardin said: 'I am unarmed!' I said: 'Go get your gun. I am armed.' Then he said: 'I'll go and get a gun and when I meet you I will come out smoking.' "

According to his story, Selman went at once to his son on the police beat, told him all about the incident and warned him to stay out of the quarrel; he also notified Police Captain Carr that he expected trouble. Then he went back to the Acme Saloon, sat down on a beerkeg outside, and waited.

"About 11 o'clock," he resumed, "Mr. Shackleford came along and insisted . . . taking a drink . . . then said 'don't get drunk.' Shackleford led me in. Hardin and Brown were shaking dice at the end of the bar near the door. While we were drinking, I noticed that Hardin watched me very closely as we went in." **(Vide)**

"When he thought my eye was off him, he made a break for his gun in his hip pocket and I immediately pulled my gun and began shooting. I shot him in the head first as I had been informed that he wore a steel breast plate. As I was about to shoot the second time, some one ran against me and I think I missed him but the other two shots were at his body and I think I hit him both times. My son ran in and caught me by the arm and said: 'He is dead. Don't shoot any more.'

"My son and myself came out of the saloon together. I was not drunk at the time but crazy mad at the way he insulted me. When Justice Howe (the coroner) came in I gave my statement to him . . . I was not placed in jail but considered myself under arrest. I am willing to stand any investigation . . . sorry I had to kill Hardin but . . . it had come to the point where either he or I had to die.' "

He neglected to mention that when the coroner saw that Wes had been shot through the back of his head, he declined to shake hands with Constable Selman.

But all amenities aside, on August 19, 1895, John Wesley Hardin met death by violence in the same way in which he had forced it on forty other men. He was buried in Concordia Cemetery at El Paso, with "Hardin's McRose" as the principal mourner, and it is assumed, without any information to contradict the assumption, that McRose appropriately faded from view.

Likewise a veil of obscurity fell around John Wesley Hardin. Fame, like quicksilver, is bright and shining, but it is unstable and may shatter and roll away past recovery. It is rare today to find anyone to whom the name John Wesley Hardin means anything.

As prescribed by law, there was an official inquest and the customery death photograph shows the body of a man in early middle age, stripped to the waist. In the faded, washed out picture, four details are impressively visible: a shock of dark hair, a luxuriant handlebar mustache, a smooth chest, and a preternaturally large right nipple. After a bullet passed through his skull, he turned in falling and another of Selman's bullets entered the right breast at the nipple, causing the exaggerated appearance.

There were four witnesses at the inquest. Henry Brown, a grocer with whom Hardin was rolling dice at the end of the bar, testified that Hardin never saw Selman, that his back was turned, that Selman shot him through the back of the head and then fired several more times. The other three witnesses were evasive or contradictory.

Three medical doctors signed a certificate that they had "examined the wounds on the person of John Wesley Hardin and that in our opinion the wound causing the death was caused by a bullet, that the bullet entered the base of the skull, **posteriorly**, and came out at the upper corner of the eye."

The somewhat unfamiliar word did not deceive the residents of El Paso. It meant that Selman had shot Hardin in the back without giving him a chance and such action under any conditions was deemed dishonorable and proscribed. Additional evidence indicated that the shooting had been pre-arranged, with assisting signals from others, including Selman's son. For a while, the town was agog with discussions pro and con, concerning Selman's justification. The arguments ceased suddenly when Selman was killed a few months later.

As a notorious gun-fighter himself, his finale was no surprise to anyone. However, Selman's record officially and personally of, alledgedly, twenty victims was paltry in comparison with Hardin's impressive score of forty.

PART

3

Sam Bass

SAM BASS GANG—Unidentified photo taken from brochure published for Sam Bass Cafe in Round Rock, Texas.

SAM BASS
1851—1878

The motorist driving south on U.S. Highway 81, will have a magnificent panorama of the Lone Star State unfolding before him. Starting at the Red River and driving the length of Texas to the Rio Grande River, he will pass the oil fields of North Texas, the industrial complex of Fort Worth-Dallas, and the rich, black land of Central Texas. He will see Austin with its great granite capitol building and the University Memorial Tower, around which the students gather.

In San Antonio, with the Spanish-Mexican influence becoming evident, he may visit the historic Alamo, dine at an open air restaurant along the river which winds through the center of the town, and possibly then catch a glimpse of the beautiful hill country to the west, where the flora and fauna are said to be the most varied in America.

Beyond San Antonio, lie the warm, arid stretches of ranch lands reaching to Laredo, Gateway to Mexico.

Let us go back, though, and pick up our motorist as he leaves Georgetown, still north of Austin. Before reaching Austin, he will pass through one more village . . . the little town of Round Rock.

Long ago there was a railroad grade crossing through Round Rock, but one foggy morning a bus filled with Baylor University basketball players collided with a freight train there and most of them were killed. Soon after, a short, high, steeply-inclined concrete overpass was built across the tracks. Atop it, all the town of Round

Rock could be seen, including its most conspicuous land mark, the old store building of native rock where Sam Bass received his fatal wounds. Directly across the street was a small building with a large sign reading "SAM BASS CAFE."

Mr. Leslie Eads, the proprietor of the cafe, served apple pie, hot from the oven, with a glass of cold milk to the hungry and curious tourists, and often presented them with a small pamphlet entitled "The True Story of Sam Bass." These were plainly marked at 10c, but Mr. Eads gave them free of charge. He even occasionally walked across the street with the tourist to point out the old doors at Koppel's General Store (then still occupied by a mercantile business), with the bullet scars made the night Sam Bass was there, and he probably would have given directions for the tourist to reach the cemetery where Sam Bass lies buried.

The visitor would have found a low bridge en route to the cemetery nothing but a ford. The tall supports of the old high bridge still stand, but the bridge itself has long since disappeared. In the middle of Brushy Creek is the large boulder from which Round Rock took its name. Intermittent floods have eroded it until it resembles a large toadstool of stone. Once the ford is crossed, we ascend a steep bank and pass through big trees crowding the creek bank and then we might think for a second that we had driven into the past century.

Here is what remains of the original Round Rock, which came to be known as Old Town. The then newly built International and Great Northern Railroad came to Round Rock declaring that its station would have to be built on higher ground, and a point was selected half a mile away. New businesses clustered around the railroad station in what came to be called New Town. But many of the houses in Old Town are remarkably well preserved. Just beyond them is the old cemetery.

No place is quite as desolate and lonely as a neglected

country graveyard, and perhaps there is no other place so likely to make us reflect on the frailty of man and his fate. Here tombstones and monuments stand askew or lie broken on the ground. Weeds and brambles choke what once were paths. One or two graves may look newer, littered with the debris of withered flowers, not yet covered with grass or weeds.

There is the unmarked grave of Sam Bass beneath a huge oak in the extreme northern corner of the cemetery, the whole of which is enclosed by a few rusty strands of barbed wire, nailed to sagging, decaying wood posts.

It is still, except for perhaps a far-off tinkling cowbell or a mockingbird. What is puzzling and memorable are the fresh flowers on the grave of Sam Bass and the clear remainder of past bouquets. Some of them are withered and in containers, other simply laid on the ground. Sam Bass has not been forgotten.

At the time of this writing, time has changed things. Highway 81 is the most heavily travelled throughway in Texas. It merely touches the edges of the larger cities and completely bypasses all the villages, including Round Rock. The old rock building where Sam Bass was shot still stands, but it has a neat coating of stucco, and the bullet-scarred doors are gone—stored away somewhere—not for sale. The present owner and his clerks have no time for interminable questions or conversations. And there is no longer a Sam Bass Cafe across the street, though there is a Sam Bass Steak House situated on the six-lane highway. The Steak House is owned and operated by Mr. H.F. Loyd, who proves as friendly and cordial as his predecessor, Mr. Eads (who closed the Sam Bass Cafe and moved to Austin). Mr. Loyd still dispenses the old pamphlets. His dwindling supply was found in an abandoned railroad store room.

"It's a strange thing," Mr. Loyd said. "Sam Bass was born more than a hundred years ago, and he was killed in

1878. But there are always fresh or new flowers on his grave. The month doesn't pass but that some person or persons put them there. It's hard to understand—but it happens, just the same."

At first glance, the old cemetery seems the same. The barbed wire fence sags a little more, and there are a few additional graves. A faded wood sign, sawn in the shape of a pointing arrow, bears the name SAM BASS—and nothing more. The big oak tree has died. But there is a new and glistening granite tombstone in the middle of the grave with the simple legend:

SAM BASS
July 21, 1851
July 21, 1878

On the grave is a wreath of roses and a vase containing asters and lillies. There are artificial flowers too, like those on the few newer graves. These tokens are only permitted in untended and unendowed cemeteries.

The cemetery is far from the roar and noise of traffic. In another tree, another mockingbird is singing the same songs which it sang for the Tejas Indians, the Spanish conquistadores, Stephen F. Austin . . . and Sam Bass.

Music is so essentially a part of our daily lives that few realize its pervasive influence. The love of musical entertainment is inherent, but most Americans of the past had to produce it on the spot. Only the most affluent could have such luxuries as a piano or foot pump-organ. Mostly in use were the fiddle, the harmonica, or French harp, an occasional banjo or mandolin and the guitar.

The usual wielder of guitar was the itinerant "hired man" and his principal mode of expression was the ballad. It was a happy day when the new hired man was brought home by the head of the family. These wandering minstrels resembled the troubadours of the middle ages and it was through such men that folk lore and folk music developed.

Long ago, in a lonely farm house when the day's work was done, a young, wandering hired man brought joy and pleasure to a small boy and his two older sisters by his singing of "Sam Bass, or The Hungry Man." (Ah, dear, wonderful Frank Bridgeman, where are you now, and what rich rewards have the years brought your way?)

His repertory covered a wide field, of past or current events, of unrequited love, or hopeful love, of personalities real or fanciful, of old hound dogs.

The original verses of the Sam Bass Ballad are said to have been written by one John Denton. The requirements for musical immortality were an attractive personality, a turn for wit, a quixotic character, and violence without brutality. In the case of Sam Bass, there was also the sympathy resulting from his base betrayal by a trusted friend. Sam Bass was a rascal who carried out his deeds in high good humor. The hired man was a milder sort of rascal, peripatetic, goodnatured, shiftless and likeable. He was not long in putting together an account of Sam Bass.

The various versions of the ballad contained many stanzas and the singers discarded those they chose to, substituting their own or others to suit themselves and their various listeners. There are scores of verses, all original and authentic, and there are variations and adaptions with allusions so limited to locality or time that their meanings are not now clear. But with the occasional difference of a word or two, all of them begin very much the same:

Sam Bass was born in Indiana
It was his native home
And at the age of seventeen
Young Sam began to roam.

Indeed Samuel Bass was born in Indiana, on July 21, 1851. His father was Daniel Bass and his mother was

Elizabeth Jane Bass. Daniel Bass was a farmer, and Sam was one of ten children.

Soon after the birth of the tenth child, his mother died. After a decent interval, Daniel Bass brought home a new wife to be stepmother to his children. The new wife was a widow with two children of her own, and in due time, she had more children by her new husband.

When Sam was ten, his father died. The farm was sold and Sam's part was put in the legal custody of his uncle, Dave Sheets. The six younger children, including Sam, were sent to this uncle to be reared.

Dave Sheets was a politician, successful, and "well-to-do." He was especially well-to-do in the matter of children, having twenty-one which were presented to him by a succession of wives. Except for the necessity of a small annex to his house, the addition of six Bass children presented no special difficulty.

The family was operated on a share-the-work basis, and each member had his appointed tasks. Sam was energetic and did his work satisfactorily. He was very popular with boys of his age—a trait which he was never to lose—but was bashful with girls and never learned to dance well despite his agility.

The operation of the Sheets menage required fairly strict regimentation. When Sam reached seventeen, his life became unbearably dull and unhappy. He wanted a horse. He wanted freedom. He wanted to come and go without having to account to his uncle. These normal desires, when expressed, were met by Dave Sheets with stern refusal. Sam countered by asking for his meager patrimony, and his uncle's blessing as well. Sheets was outraged.

So Sam, advising only his favorite and understanding sister, Sally, took his leave. He had decided to go to Texas and lead the exciting life of a cowboy. As can be imagined, this presented problems. He had no money and had to work his way painfully and slowly in a southerly and westerly direction. It is only fair to state that Dave Sheets did eventually send Sam's inheritance to him, but not until Sam was twenty.

In time, Sam had reached Rosedale, Mississippi. It was a river-boat town, busy and raucous, a point of departure for men and families leaving the crowded East to seek fortunes in the West. It was here Sam got his first knowledge of gambling.

An old tin-type made about the time Sam must have been planning his departure from home, and belonging to his sister, Sally, showed a boy with somewhat formless features, but with the undeniable beauty which is youth.

He had no trouble finding work in Rosedale and he soon became acquainted with a boy named Scott Mayes, who with his parents, was on the way to Texas. Mr. and Mrs. Mayes were taken with the orphan boy, and his slow smile and boundless energy. It was agreed that Sam would accompany them in their overland journey to Denton, Texas. They travelled in a covered wagon. (Sam had a brother named Denton, and it is likely the destination seemed auspicious to him.)

> He first came out to Texas
> A cowboy for to be
> A kinder hearted fellow
> You seldom ever see . . . .

From Rosedale, Mississippi to Denton, Texas by air is a flight of less than two hours. It was, however, for the Mayes and their new protege, several months later in the autumn, when they reached their destination. Sam learned that cowhands were wanted on the Caruth ranch, south of Denton, and he applied for a job there and was hired.

It took only one Texas winter, with its sudden "Northers" and chilling rains to convince him that all the glamour of a cowpoke's life exists only in the imaginations of those who haven't experienced it. Besides, Sam was used to the commotion and company of a large family. He was only too happy to get back to Denton the following spring.

He found a job at once with Mrs. Lacy, the kind, wise lady, we are told, who operated Denton's finest hostelry, The Lacy House. Sam was general factotum. His duties included handling and stabling the guests' horses, a difficult and exacting chore.

Mrs. Lacy was fond of Sam and bragged on him so often that he received another offer, and Mrs. Lacy was delighted, because it meant a step upward for him. His new employer was "Dad" Egan, a man of means and prestige. In addition to local interests, "Dad" Egan owned several farms, and operated freight lines between Denton, Fort Worth, Dallas, Sherman and other North Texas settlements.

Sam did whatever needed doing. He particularly liked freighting, with its travel and variety. His expense accounts were so modest that Mr. Egan suspected he was feeding himself and the horses too sparingly.

The Egans treated Sam as a member of the family, and there is an abundance of evidence that they remained fond of him even when he fell from grace.

Sam made many friends. One was tall, handsome Frank Jackson, who worked in the tin shop. He was five years younger than Sam, and would remain Sam's most admiring and devoted friend. Another friend was saturnine Henry Underwood. And then there was Jim Murphy, the friend who would betray Sam and cause his death.

This was probably the happiest time in his life, but he had one consuming passion. He longed to have his own horse. He saved his money, carefully and stingily. It was not just any old horse he wanted. It had to be something special.

He made a deal in race stock
One called the "Denton Mare"
He matched her in scrub races
And took her to the fair.

Sam saw his "dream horse" at last, when he passed the hitching post near the hotel and spied a filly tied there. A female Pegasus, or at least a daughter of Bucephalus! Beside himself with excitement, he lost no time in seeking out the owner, but to his dismay, the owner wanted twice as much as Sam could pay. But Sam was a powerful persuader, even when so young and still without a gun, and he persuaded Dad Egan's younger brother to buy a half-interest with him. So he acquired the filly, "Jenny," in partnership. It was never his intention to waste her as a riding horse. Jenny was to become a race horse.

Dad Egan let Sam keep Jenny in his own stables, and Sam spent long, painstaking, weary hours in training her for the races. Competing horses were not handicapped then by weighting; all that was necessary was that the horse be ridden by someone. As a jockey, Sam selected and trained a diminutive black boy named Dick. For Dick, a saddle was just excess baggage, and Jenny was not even burdened with a bridle. Instead a hackamore was used, which is a light rope passed around the horse's neck and through his mouth. Dick was the Eddie Arcaro of his day. With Dick up, Jenny never lost a race.

A racetrack in Sam's day was any suitable, level straight-away stretch of land. Spectators, standing or on horses, marked the side boundaries. The length of the track was usually not more than a quarter-mile. Rules were made for the specific occasion, and decisions by the judges were final. Occasionally, the decisions were very final, but only for the judges. There were no stewards, detectives or officials to maintain order and decorum, consequently bribing, "fixing," and other irregularities were the rule.

Dad Egan had political ambitions, and since he well knew of the abuses connected with horse-racing, he found it prudent to require his brother to sell his interest in Jenny to Sam, advanced Sam the necessary funds, and permitted Jenny to remain a boarder in his stables.

As Mr. Egan feared, Sam soon got into a great deal of trouble with disgruntled losers and with law-enforcement authorities. It became increasingly difficult to find anyone in the locality who was foolish enough to match a horse against the "Denton Mare." (Usually the stake was money, but sometimes it was the losing horse, or other horses.)

Sam took Jenny up to the Indian Territory and legitimately won a number of ponies. But the Indians, as losers, exhibited the same reversible attitudes which characterized them as givers, and they refused to release the ponies. The situation eventually became so unsatisfactory and difficult that Mr. Egan regretfully advised Sam their association could not continue. They parted the best of friends, and Sam set forth with his horse in search of new worlds to conquer.

The results, financially, were irregular and disappointing, until, in San Antonio, Sam met up with a former Denton acquaintance named Joel Collins. Joel was an experienced trail driver, who had just opened a saloon in San Antonio. He was more riotous, quarrelsome and violent than any of his customers, and he drank much more. The saloon was not a success, understandably, and he and Sam, almost immediately, "teamed up."

> Sam used to coin the money
> And spent it just as free
> He always drank good whiskey
> Wherever he might be

Under the influence of the older and more experienced Joel Collins, Sam now departed permanently from the paths of righteousness.

Jenny played the principal part in the deceptions and frauds which followed. The main trick was a variation of the old "Ringer" race horse fraud. In a community where racing was a popular pastime, Joel Collins would appear: a typical citizen with a dejected looking mare. He would proclaim in a most unprofessional manner that he had recently sold his cattle and wanted to get on the race track circuit.

The mare, under various names, would appear dejected because she was carefully kept away from currycomb, brush and file. Occasionally she was given an application of walnut oil, or other ointment, to change her color and make her appear an even more unlikely winner.

Then, a few days before the race, a prosperous looking, convivial Sam Bass would blow into town. Skillfully seeking out talkative citizens, he would confide that the fellow with the mare was a stupid dolt who had accidentally made some money, and that the kindest lesson which could be given him was to relieve him of the money. Sam would say that he had seen the mare run, and that she was a sorry excuse for a race horse—a dog, a mere nag, a "plater" that was always left at the post.

There were no racing forms or handicap sheets for study and Sam was a most convincing talker. Bets on Jenny by her owner were gleefully taken up, and long odds given. The money poured in—and out just as quickly.

Sam always managed to disappear before the race. But there was a limit to the gullibility of the public, and the trick could never be repeated in the same place.

There was no question that Sam liked whiskey. Then, as now, it was the most efficient lubricant for a quick-starting, smooth-running acquaintance. Sam could hold his liquor, and most of the gamblers he searched out were found in and around the popular saloons.

In any case, the pickings grew slim at the same time the

grass grew green and the air balmy, signaling the time of year for the cattle drive.

Joel Collins had a brother named Joe, who was an industrious and successful rancher. The brothers, in fact, though their names were similar, were completely different in character. But Joel Collins had driven cattle up the trail four times, and since his brother, Joe, had a herd to take to market, Joel persuaded Sam that they should join him. Jenny was sold to provide a grubstake.

> Sam left the Collins ranch
> In the merry month of May
> With a herd of Texas cattle
> For the Black Hills far away

The grassy Texas prairies teemed with cattle, but there was as yet no railroad to transport them to the beef-hungry North and East, and the common practice was to drive them overland to a railroad point. Trail driving required a knowledge of topography and horsemanship, and of humans and cattle as well. It also required a strong constitution. Several trails were well-known. A rancher named Chisum sold cattle to the Indian agencies, and used a loosely defined route for his deliveries.

Further north, a half-breed Cherokee Indian, Jesse Chisolm, guided and assisted Federal soldiers in re-occupying posts along the Washita River, and in so doing, laid out additional routes. The whole complex, consolidated by connecting routes, came to be known, loosely, as The Chisolm Trail.

The terminal point of the Chisolm Trail was Abilene, Kansas. There, J.G. McCoy conducted a stockyard and marketing operation, tremendous even by contemporary standards. More than 700,000 head of livestock went through Abilene in 1871.

(Later, the fame of Abilene would dim, but would once

more be remembered as the childhood home of Dwight David Eisenhower.)

The trail taken by Sam Bass, Joel Collins and three other drivers lay to the west of the Chisolm Trail, and its terminus was Dodge City, Iowa, further north. They drove a herd of 700 beeves, of which 150 came from Joe Collins' ranch.

(The similarity of names caused confusion in the history of Sam Bass, and where, in the ballad, Joe Collins is named, it should have been Joel.)

Sold out at Custer City
And then got on a spree
A jollier lot of cowboys
You seldom ever see

The drive ended successfully, and in Dodge City, Sam and Joel heard of "gold in the Black Hills . . . easy to pick up." Today, the real treasure is in the Williston Basin. It is liquid, it is black, it is oil. But in Sam's time, it was gold.

The center of activity was Deadwood, South Dakota, and there never existed a more riotous, lawless, wide-open frontier town. Even the name was sinister. Had there been a chamber of commerce, it would have had to admit these town statistics: Saloons 75, Churches 0.

There, Sam might have glimpsed Kitty LeRoy, Martha Jane Canary (Calamity Jane), and other famous "frontier ladies."

When they arrived in Deadwood it had already become too cold in the Black Hills for any actual prospecting, and they turned to gambling, at which they considered themselves proficient. They found they were amateurs when pitted against the real professionals.

Then a freighting trip lost money. It looked to be a long, hard winter.

Until then, Sam's most serious breach had been cheating at the races, a situation in which it was simply every man for himself. Now, under the influence of Joel Collins and the pressure of circumstance, Sam and Joel resorted to robbing stage coaches. There were seven such robberies, and they served merely as a warming-up for the more substantial undertaking of robbing the Union Pacific Express.

On their way back to Texas
They robbed the U.P. train
And then split up in couples
And started out again

Many may remember the isolated railroad water towers of the past, although none are now to be seen. The iron horse, like his counterpart, required frequent watering and the towers were spaced at regular intervals along the line, many of them far from human habitation. At such a remote tank, called Big Springs, Nebraska, on the night of September 19, 1877, the eastbound Union Pacific Express ground to a stop for the customary purpose. Joel Collins, Bill Heffridge, Jim Berry, Tom Nixon, Jack Davis, and Sam Bass lay in wait.

Whether the six knew the train carried a valuable cargo, or whether they were there to take pot luck, is not known. It may have been coincidence that in the express car's heavy safe was $200,000. Unfortunately, the safe defied their attempts to open it, but fortunately, there was other valuable cargo: three small, wooden boxes, each neatly closed with red sealing wax, each containing one thousand newly minted twenty-dollar gold pieces from California. A nice, heavy box for each pair of the robbers.

In addition to the fortune inside the safe which the robbers were unable to obtain, a considerable amount of silver bars had to be left behind because they were too heavy to transport.

But they had their $20,000 per box, and the passengers

were required to "shell out." During that part of the robbery, when Sam noticed that a one-armed passenger had been robbed, he apologetically returned the man's money.

> Joe Collins and his partner
> Were overtaken soon
> With all their stolen money
> They had to meet their doom

It seems probable that the Union Pacific train job was planned and engineered by someone with considerably more experience than Sam Bass, the novice, would have had. A shrewd part of the plan had been the pairing off afterward of the bandits who then took separate routes. Joel Collins took Hefferidge as his partner.

Robbery of the United States mails was, of course, a Federal offense. The Army was called in immediately and a detachment of the Tenth Cavalry overtook and killed Collins and Hefferidge in a gun battle at Buffalo, Kansas. The second pair, Nixon and Berry, rode east, sedulously trailed, without their knowledge, by an amateur sleuth. Appropriately enough, the name of this embryonic Holmes was Leech. He was able to direct officers to Berry, who was killed near his own home in Mexico, Missouri. Nixon managed to escape, presumably to Canada. In due time, Leech was rewarded for his persistence with part of the $10,000 reward.

But Sam Bass and his partner, Jack Davis, had no trouble whatsoever in deceiving and eluding pursuers. Sam and Jack were both very young men and it probably seemed unlikely to the authorities that a robbery on so grand a scale could have been pulled off by any except older and experienced hands. In any case, Sam and Jack made no effort toward concealment. They acquired somehow a rickety old surrey and a couple of nags, and drove leisurely toward Texas. The gold was carried in sacks, like so many potatoes; crowded in among the miscellaneous paraphernalia and supplies which two lads travelling through the country might be expected to have with them.

> Sam made it back to Texas
> All right side up with care
> Rode into the town of Denton
> With all his friends to share

Their pleasant journey ended at Fort Worth. Davis bought a railroad ticket for New Orleans, and disappeared. Sam bought himself a pony and for a while lingered in Fort Worth.

Hard money, particularly gold, was the preferred medium of exchange, and a man spending twenty dollar gold pieces did not attract undue attention.

Sam was a little reluctant about returning to Denton. The fact that "Dad" Egan had become Sheriff of Denton County complicated matters. Eventually, he could resist no more and went back, where he spent his gold pieces liberally. He was an easy touch. When friends commented on his generosity, he replied enigmatically, and with a smile, that he had struck it rich up north.

In Wise and Cooke Counties, Texas, there once was a large area of wilderness called Cove Hollow. Today, oil derricks and houses dot the landscape, and highways crisscross it, making it hard to believe that it was once a strange and impenetrable densely wooded canyon. Part of this area, the canyon included, lay about forty-three miles northwest of Denton. Its briars and bushes, oak and walnut trees, make it a secluded haven for such as would wish so lonely a retreat. Visitors were quite unlikely. Even intrepid officers of the law would have hesitated to enter such a trackless labyrinth. It had irresistible advantages to offer Sam Bass as a possible retreat in time of trouble, and he decided to make it his base for future operations. Jim Murphy, one of his old friends, lived with a brother in a small house near Cove Hollow, and Sam frequently visited them. It soon happened that the most reliable way of getting in touch with Sam was to leave a message for him with Jim Murphy.

Sam Bass had four companions
Each a bold and daring lad
Jim Murphy, Jackson, Underwood
Joe Collins—and old "Dad."

Although he was plentifully supplied with money, Sam was becoming bored with the inactive life. He contacted his friend Underwood, who was himself constantly running afoul of the law. We must assume Sam took Underwood into his confidence and that they discussed the future, because Underwood soon left his wife and family to join Sam.

Sam Bass wasn't a ladies' man, but the kind of man who fascinated other men, for many of them left kith and kin to join him for long or short periods of time. His favorite friend seemed to be Frank Jackson, who would later demonstrate his loyalty. Frank, several years younger than Sam, gave him a kind of hero worship, dating from the time that Sam had let him proudly ride the Denton Mare. Frank was persuaded to join Sam and Underwood, and, in November of 1877, the trio set out for a gay old time in San Antonio.

The first stop was Fort Worth. It had been a trail drive town, and was now in boomtimes. A handsome new granite court house was going up at the head of Main Street, near the site of the original fort. In Fort Worth, Sam outfitted his friends with mounts, clothing and fire arms. Account records of the old A.J. Anderson Gun Store, (recently liquidated), show that Sam bought three hundred and sixty dollars worth of guns and ammunition, a considerable sum at the time, and that the money was paid in twenty-dollar gold pieces. The sale was the first of the size made by the owner of the new gun store, and was meticulously recorded in the ledger.

Sam and his friends reached San Antonio in December. At that time, it more nearly resembled a Mexican town, and it was thronged with travellers. There were many photographers. It is not likely there was anyone to whom Sam would have wanted to send a photograph of himself, and there were obvious reasons why he would have preferred not to have been photographed at all, but a photograph taken of three men in San Antonio about that time is extant and is alleged to be of Sam Bass and his two companions.

The art of the photographer in the Seventies was long and difficult. The camera usually was a cumbersome apparatus, covered with a black drop-cloth under which the photographer stuck his head to view the subject through the lens. Frequently, there was a fanciful painted background. The subject was posed and required to remain immobile for some length of time. To assure his cooperation, iron clamps were firmly adjusted to the head and other parts of the body, hidden from view.

The inevitable result was a glum, unhappy, or even menacing expression. The alleged photograph of Sam and friends shows them in a setting which appears to be the ruins of Rome. The seated central figure—supposedly Sam—holds a pistol and is flanked on both sides by ridiculous-looking desperados. The smaller of these has a slanting bandolier across his middle, and the other brigand, a huge man, stands as if confident his brute strength can cope with any eventuality. Over luxuriant mustaches they glower with fixed, and slightly dazed expressions. One has a squint and may be slightly crosseyed. The group looks like the robbers from a Keystone cop comedy, but the central figure, on whose shoulders rests an affectionate hand from each of the partners, has tried for composed dignity. He is debonair and good-looking. He came through the ordeal with flying colors.

A smudged reproduction of this picture appears in the Round Rock pamphlet and a better copy can be seen at the Witte Museum in San Antonio.

Unfortunately, it isn't likely this is a picture of Sam Bass. DuVal West, now deceased, former United States District Judge, had tentatively identified the central figure as a felon who passed through his court for sentencing on a robbery conviction; his name now forgotten. From the result of long and diligent search, the author must conclude that there is no existing authentic picture of Sam Bass, the man. The only authentic likeness of him is that faded tintype taken in his younger years, which belonged to his sister, Sally. Nevertheless, it is possible to piece together a reasonably clear picture of how Sam Bass looked.

One biographer offered these statistics: "He was five feet eight inches, with a slight stoop, firm of muscle, with sallow skin, dark hair and eyes. He looked like he had a strain of Indian in him. He had a downcast look and drawled out his words in a high-pitched nasal twang. He wore old clothes, loafed and whittled around the Ēgan house."

A "Wanted" poster described him thus: "five feet seven inches high, black hair, brown mustached, large white teeth, shows them when talking." It concludes with disappointment, "Has little to say."

Still other snatches of glimpses:

"A good-humored no-count teamster who trailed shrewd, unscrupulous Joe Collins around San Antonio."

"A fine rider and a crack shot, a devil-may-care fellow."

"There was something about him you couldn't resist. He could talk you into anything . . . he could be still or make you laugh like anything." This last testimony came from a Denton acquaintance.

There is no doubt that Sam was of less than average height. Many great men of history have been. Psychologists explain that the smaller man, unable to meet others on an eye-to-eye level, is compelled to demonstrate that he is equal to all, and "more equal" than most. There is no evidence, however, that Sam suffered either these compulsions or frustrations. Nor, of course, is he to be considered a "great man," except in his particular and limited field, and then with the understanding that "greatness" connotates neither good nor bad, and that few in his profession ever attained his stature, even posthumously.

He had little formal education, and although he could read enough for practical purposes, he could barely write. His letters from Denton were written for him by Charlie Brim, and the few letters he posted from other places were undoubtedly penned for him by anyone who was willing and at hand.

Unknown to these three cowboys on a spree, they had been trailed to San Antonio by the Sheriff of Grayson County, and by a Deputy Sheriff from Denton County. The Sheriff was convinced that Underwood was really the Nixon who had robbed the Union Pacific in South Dakota, and the Deputy Sheriff, knowing Underwood had a solid alibi for that crime, was after him on a completely different charge. Neither Sheriff nor Deputy Sheriff knew of the other's pursuit. When they accidentally met on the streets in San Antonio, a loud and violent argument resulted, which was overheard by "a lady of the streets," who wasted no time in reporting it to Sam Bass. He and his companions hurried out of town, so the story goes.

After long days of riding, the urgent alarms of San Antonio must have grown to seem far away, and they began to feel the need of challenge and excitement. Nine miles west of Fort Worth, at Mary's Creek, the opportunity appeared. (This area is now a beautiful suburb of Fort Worth, filled with the well-manicured lawns and sparkling residences of oil millionaires.)

Heavy rains and high water had delayed the Cleburne stage coach, but when it finally appeared at 1:00 A.M.,

Sam and his friends delayed it a bit longer. Only one frightened passenger "shelled out," a paltry twenty-three dollars. The others claimed they had nothing to give. Sam knew that most of them had considerable sums hidden on their persons, but he permitted nothing so degrading as an intimate search. He contented himself with a remark that was to become famous: "This country," he announced to the assembly, "is going to the dogs. Nothing but poor white trash riding in coaches nowadays!"

The trio struck again on January 26, 1878. This time it was in a ravine west of Mary's Creek, and midway between Fort Worth and Weatherford. Before the robbery, a chance traveller had been stopped by the three men, told what was going to happen, and allowed to remain, or forced to remain, as the case may have been, to watch. He later described the proceeding in detail. The robbers tied handkerchiefs around their faces, with holes cut out for their eyes. When the stage came down into the ravine, the driver was confronted by rifles and six-shooters, and stopped the coach. The passengers were ordered out.

The first to alight was Valentine Werner, who was architect for the new Tarrant County court house. He was a "tenderfoot" and may be forgiven his justifiable agitation as he cried out:

"For God's sake, don't shoot!" and passed over his money and gold watch.

The operation proceeded and after a quick appraisal, Sam saw the yield was slightly under four hundred dollars. It was the largest amount he had yet taken in a stage coach robbery, and he became lyrical: "Robbing the stages, pays poor wages."

Apparently, Sam Bass had a quixotic ideal: his victims should be honest with him. But even when they were not, he was considerate and courteous with them. He knew what it was to be broke and friendless in a strange country, and he often saw to it that passengers were left with sufficient money to tide them over until they could be in touch with friends or relatives.

Charles Russell, the great American artist who captured the spirit of the Old West on canvas, painted a picture of a stage coach robbery which followed, in almost precise detail, the holdup at Mary's Creek. The principal difference, according to the late Sid Richardson who left a multi-million dollar collection of Russells and Remingtons, is that the directing bandit in the Russell picture is supposed to have been an individual known as Big Nose George. Frederick Remington, technically an even better artist, painted a canvas titled "A Dash for Timber," which portrays, in two of the mounted figures, the last fatal ride of Sam Bass.

Sam Bass, we know, loved horses and was an expert horseman. He understood both the capabilities and the limitations of the animal. In addition, he was a natural-born woodsman and plainsman. He could travel back to his hideout so quickly after a robbery that it seemed impossible he could have been the perpetrator.

Frequently, he, Frank Jackson, and another crony or two, would ride into Denton. This usually took place around sundown or later, and they were not molested. In keeping with the times, they would "whoop it up," visiting saloons, yelling and shouting and shooting their pistols, and eventually riding off in clouds of dust in an answering noise of barking dogs and crying, frightened children.

Remembering the rich haul from the Union Pacific robbery, and considering that "robbing stages pays poor wages," Sam decided to turn his hand again to train robberies. Such an undertaking required more manpower than he had available, so he passed the word that he would welcome recruits for the enterprise, and they were not long in applying. He was most exacting in his requirements.

One recruit was considered most promising. He was several years Sam's junior, and was named "Seaborn Barnes." He was called "Seab," and also had the strange nickname of "Nubbins Colt." Barnes had been involved in a shooting scrape when he was only seventeen, and had festered in jail a year before being brought to trial. And then he was acquitted. Perhaps his willingness to join Sam's group is better understood in the light of this background.

At any rate, with a skilled force, Sam Bass was ready for action.

Sam's life was short in Texas
Three robberies did he do
He robbed all of the passengers
Express and mail cars too

The balladeer is in error again. There were four train robberies, and Sam seldom resorted in them again to the lengthy process of robbing passengers.

The first of these was the robbery of the Houston and Texas Central at Allen Station, between Dallas and McKinney. With Sam were Jackson, Barnes, and another cohort, never identified. On Washington's Birthday in 1878 the four men rode near the station and under cover of darkness tied their horses in a nearby clump of trees. The train, as usual, was late and when the whistle was finally heard, the bandits surprised and tied up the station master and his assistant. Then when the train pulled in and stopped, its engineer and fireman were captured and given the same treatment.

Approximately $1,400.00 was taken from the express car, but no attempt was made to rob the passengers who no doubt were frantically engaged in hiding their money and jewelry. Several shots were fired in the melee, but no one was wounded or killed. The bold robbery caused intense excitement, and Governor Hubbard offered $500.00 rewards for the capture of the culprits.

Subsequent robberies followed this same pattern. After

nightfall the masked bandits would hide their horses near a railway station and when the train came in, the operators, guards and passengers were held at gun-point. The highly efficient robbers knew what they were looking for and exactly where to look to get it.

The second robbery took place at Hutchins, a station eight miles south of Dallas on March 18, 1878, and again the Houston and Texas Central Railway was the corporate victim. Less than $500.00 was taken that time, and some of the passengers took potshots at the robbers. But the bandits were soon safely back at their retreat in the Trinity or Hickory Creek bottoms. The Bass Gang were the prime suspects, and posses were organized to try to locate them.

Only three weeks later a third train robbery occurred at Eagle Ford (now absorbed into the metroplex) just six miles west of Dallas. No shots were fired, and a mere $140.00 was the loss of the Texas and Pacific Railroad. The names of Bass and his associates were published as suspects, but no charges were filed against them.

The fourth hold-up was at Mesquite, just east of Dallas, where a Texas and Pacific passenger train was the victim. About $150.00 was stolen. The station master, J.K. Zurn, was being visited by his wife at the time when they were locked up in the depot. Later the couple moved to Fort Worth and became prominent citizens there.

Sam had another helper
Called Arkansas for short.

In planning his robberies, Sam Bass varied the number and personnel of his gang, either because of availability or for purposes of deception. There were always volunteer recruits and among them was Arkansas Johnson. Though it sounds ridiculous, it was said that Johnson had escaped from jail by use of a small saw which his wife had brought him in a pound of butter. At first Sam was not too impressed with his skills, but later found him useful and apparently included him in one or more of the train robberies.

The public had become thoroughly aroused and alarmed. Dallas and Denton were growing frontier cities and their citizens were concerned about this rash of crime. The railroads demanded protection and the newspapers added their powerful influence. The situation was obviously beyond the control of local authorities, and the Governor directed action.

> Four of the boldest cowboys
> The ranges ever knew
> They whipped the Texas Rangers
> And ran the boys in blue.

In Denton charges were filed against Sam Bass and his confederates, and presumably the warrants were given to Sheriff Egan for service.

Against Sam Bass were arrayed Major Jones and his Frontier Batallion of Texas, all of the United States Marshalls in Texas, all city and county peace officers, William Pinkerton, with a corp of Chicago detectives, hired by the Texas Express Company, and countless volunteers. To add to all this, the Governor created at Dallas another Special Ranger Troop of thirty, and commissioned Junius (June) Peak as Lieutenant in command. Peak was thirty-three at the time. He did not wish to accept the commission, saying that some of the suspects were friends, and "belonged to the same church." A tintype photograph shows Peak, with two enormous pistols hanging from his belt, and leaning on a Winchester, in a room with tasseled draperies, chair and table.

Peak was a highly respected man, and after he accepted the commission, the first battle of the Bass War went to him.

One of three applicants for service with Sam Bass was

named Billie Scott. He was rejected while the other two men were accepted. In a fit of rage, reportedly, Scott went to Lieutenant Peak and revealed the names of the two accepted men. They were captured, prosecuted for complicity in one of the robberies, and sent to prison for life. (Later they were pardoned by President Cleveland after surviving voluntary service on a plague ship anchored outside New York harbor.)

Lieutenant Peak's initial success spurred on the chase, and feeling ran high that the matter would soon be ended.

Sheriff Egan would not or could not locate Sam. The principal form of weekend amusement became the organizing of posses. Detectives of amateur and professional standing, some with false whiskers, swarmed in and around Dallas. Posses frequently fired on one another. Fort Worth may have been a little less hostile to Sam, as he spent some of his money there.

The occasion actually arose when Sam sent word that he was tired and in need of rest. A short truce was declared.

Excitement ran high in Denton when Lt. Peak arrived there April 30th with twenty-seven men. With the assistance of Sheriff Egan, every possible man was pressed into service. Rumors of encounters began to come from every direction, while Sam and his men hid in the Cove Hollow swamps for several weeks.

In one of his rare mistakes, Sam was caught between a detachment of Rangers and a posse. Arkansas Johnson was killed. On him was found his pistol and a total of thirty-five cents. Many claimed to have fired the shot, but Ranger Tom Floyd was given official credit.

> Tom is a big six-footer
> And thinks he's mighty fly
> But I'll tell you his racket
> He's a deadbeat on the sly

At one time, Sheriff Egan passed a short distance from Sam's men, but Sam would not permit him to be shot. The

Sheriff's wife later returned the courtesy when Sam and Frank Jackson rode into Denton one day to recover two horses which a posse had captured. At the livery stable, Sam ordered the horses saddled and when the hostler refused, Frank hit him with a pistol. Sam remonstrated with Frank, ordered him to saddle the horses, and handed the hostler a gold piece. In their dash from town they passed Sheriff Egan's house. The sheriff was asleep upstairs, as Sam waved at Mrs. Egan. She later explained she could not wake her husband because he was too tired from having been out all night chasing Sam Bass.

On a morning after that, Sam and his friends reined up at Pilot Knob to buy supplies. A neighborhood posse was formed and word sent to Sheriff Egan. Other squads rushed to the spot and there was much shooting but Sam, after leading them to a point near Fort Worth, slipped away again.

"Late one evening at the Perry Roe ranch, about seven miles west of Palo Pinto, two travellers knocked on the door and were admitted by Mrs. Mahala Roe. The spokesman introduced himself as "Mr. Hampton." He wore a gray suit and floppy hat. The strangers were tired and asked Mrs. Roe for a night's lodging. Only Mrs. Roe and her two daughters were in the house and her daughters happened to be Mrs. Byron Maddox and Mrs. R.W. Maddox. The men were away helping to build a community church.

Since hospitality under almost any conditions was assured in Texas, Mrs. Roe invited them to stay and prepared supper for them. After the meal, she showed them to the best room, with a four-poster bed, put a lamp on the dresser, and told them goodnight. However, Mrs. Roe and her daughters, discussing the situation in the next room, were frightened. Mrs. Roe went to the woodshed and brought in an axe, but obviously this did not allay her fear, because she next took down a shotgun. Then she remembered that the shells for the gun were in a trunk in the room occupied by the visitors. She was a woman of action, and she knocked on their door. It was opened at once, and all concerned were surprised. On the bed lay a number of guns, and, on the dresser, a Bowie knife.

Mrs. Roe asked the visitors for their guns. "I think as gentlemen you should turn those guns over to us. We are defenseless."

But "Mr. Hampton" refused, apologetically. He told Mrs. Roe that he and his companions were hunted men, and that all that stood between them and death were their guns. He assured Mrs. Roe that she and her daughters were safe, but the resolute Mrs. Roe marched to the trunk and filled her apron with shotgun shells.

It was a sleepless night for all at the ranch house, as was sheepishly admitted the next morning. The guests ate breakfast with relish and left a twenty dollar gold piece on the table. The ladies were thanked and again assured that their visitors would have defended them with their own lives."

When the husbands returned, they realized from their wives' accounts of the event that Sam Bass and associates had been there. They were prepared to take out after the gang, but the women reminded them that they had had a memorable experience, and that twenty dollars had been most generous payment, and the men desisted.

Many years later at Palo Pinto in an interview for the **Fort Worth Star-Telegram,** Mrs. Byron Maddox recalled, "They were perfect gentlemen."

Except for the above mentioned women, the faithful sister, Sally, Mrs. Mayes of the covered wagon, Mrs. Lacy, the first employer at Denton, Mrs. Egan, the wife of the sheriff, Mrs. Zurn, the station agent's wife at Mesquite, and the mysterious "lady of the street," in San Antonio, no other women appear in most authentic accounts of the life of Sam Bass.

Sam and his band were next encountered on the Palo Pinto Road near Caddo, Texas, by the Sheriff's men and a group of Texas Rangers. Fifty shots were fired: no one was hurt.

It is reported that soon afterward, Sam's men captured a few of the posse. There was a supply of liquor and considerable fraternization is said to have occurred. When Sam and his crew departed, their erstwhile chasers were left high in spirits, but low in locomotive ability. On another occasion, it was rumored that the Rangers located their quarry in a cedar brake but were unable to make the capture.

The Rangers, not surprisingly, had become tired of the whole, aimless, futile business. They claimed they had enlisted to fight Indians and Mexicans—not fellow-Texans, and most of them resigned and turned in their equipment which was forwarded to "June" Peak.

The Bass War was almost ended. Sam had lost Arkansas Johnson and two of his recruits. Jim Murphy had unaccountably disappeared.

The only casualty among their pursuers (aside from saddle sores and wrenched backs) occurred at Denton when one of the posse accidentally shot off his own toe.

There is a reasonably authenticated and detailed account of Sam's last months. The reporter was Jim Murphy who talked endlessly to all who would listen.

After the senseless activity of the "Bass War," train robberies were obviously too risky and were, in any case, disappointingly unprofitable. The Union Pacific Express had carried an enormous sum, but that proved to be an exceptional case. Of course, Sam was no economist. He did not realize that the growth of banking and the practices of exchange and credits, made unnecessary the actual transfer of large sums of money. But he did know that for whatever reason, money was now in banks. His supply of gold pieces was dwindling. The expected result was his decision to make banks the object of their efforts, as he and his men "worked" their way south toward

Mexico and retirement.

According to stories, Sam had been badly shaken by the death of Arkansas Johnson. Now Underwood decided he would go his separate way, and so did two of the newer members of the gang. And so it was only Sam, Seab Barnes and ever-faithful Frank Jackson who rode back to the comparative security of Cove Hollow to rest and to plan.

The entire proceeds of the two stage-coach hold ups and four train robberies, from December of 1877 through April of 1878 was $1961.00.

Jim Murphy was arrested
And then released on bail
He jumped his bond at Tyler
And took the train for Terrell

Jim Murphy had been arrested and jailed for complicity in the train robberies. He appears to have been a man of unstable character. On occasion, he had acted as go-between for Sam and the law, and he vacillated between his contempt for the law, and his fear of it. Knowing this, or at least suspecting it, Major Jones and Captain Peak of the Rangers selected Jim Murphy as their means to an end. The agreement was simply that Murphy would betray Sam to them, turn State's evidence, and in turn be granted immunity.

Accordingly, ostensibly, Murphy was released on bail, and the story was circulated that he had jumped bailbond. Murphy was to return to Denton, locate Sam and his friends, and deliver them over to the Rangers by pre-arrangement.

But Major Jones had posted Jim
And that was all a stall
'T'was only a plan to capture Sam
Before the coming fall.

Within two or three days, Murphy succeeded in finding Sam, relating his story of having jumped bond, and accepting their invitation to rejoin Sam's expedition South. As the journey began, it was Murphy's bad luck to be thrown from his horse and injured. The band left him behind to recover and it took him two weeks to locate them again. He had no choice then but to rejoin them and hope he could get word to Jones and Peak about their plans.

It is largely from reports Murphy made to the Rangers, and his statements afterward, when Sam had been betrayed and killed, that the story of the last weeks are pieced together.

Murphy's work had been cut out for him. The outlaw band had no travel plan, no particular itinerary. Mails were slow and unreliable and Murphy had few chances to mail letters. Members of the band were seldom separated. To add to these problems, Seab Barnes watched him warily and continually. He had been suspicious of Murphy from the beginning, and supposedly had been told that Murphy was a traitor.

>
> Jim had used Sam's money
> And didn't want to pay
> He thought his only chance was
> To give poor Sam away

It was difficult for Sam Bass to believe that someone he had befriended and treated generously could be guilty of treachery. He had lent Murphy a considerable amount of money and it was possible that Murphy simply wanted to eliminate his creditor. When Murphy discovered that he was supected he was, in his own words, "scared to death," and realized that he would have to be extremely careful in trying to communicate with the Rangers.

Barnes had not been convinced of Murphy's innocence,

despite Jackson's efforts. On the night following the confrontation, when the party camped at the edge of Rockwall, Texas, Barnes rode into the town to buy canned peaches. While he was gone, Sam spied a gallows standing some distance away. It had been used in an execution and had not been dismantled. He walked over to it and examined it carefully.

"Well, boys," he said, "that's the first one of those things I ever seen. And I hope it's the last."

The next stop was Kaufman. As usual, camp was made outside the town, but the band rode in to town together for the luxury of being barbered, and they bought new suits. They also bought more canned peaches. The largest and most prosperous store in town could not change a twenty-dollar gold piece, and they had to buy more than they intended.

They crossed the Trinity River at Trinidad. According to Murphy, they met and talked with many of the country people and other wanderers as well and while they used fictitious names, they made no particular effort at hiding. Sam even conducted a popularity poll of sorts, by guiding conversations to Sam Bass. He found out he had more admirers than enemies.

When they reached Waco, a bustling and prosperous town, the bank there offered a most promising prospect. Murphy, however, was desperate. He feared he would be implicated in a robbery and that then the Rangers would think he had switched allegiance again. At their camp that night he used all his powers of persuasion to discourage the Waco bank prospect. He pointed out that Waco was a large town, a county seat with many officers, on a well-travelled road, and in a flat country which afforded little protection. He proposed that they go further south to the hill country, and rob the Williamson County Bank at Round Rock.

Sam agreed. But they made one more trip into Waco, and Sam and Murphy stopped at the Ranch Saloon. Sam jingled a gold coin on the counter. "There goes the last 77 gold piece," he said, referring to the year of the Union Pacific hold-up, and the mint date of the coin. "It hasn't done me much good. But we'll soon get us some more."

At Belton, Texas, Murphy finally managed to post a letter to the Sheriff at Sherman, Texas, telling him that Sam Bass and his gang were planning to rob the bank at Round Rock. This was on July 13, 1878.

They crossed the Lampasas River and reached Georgetown, where they lingered for a day and did a little shopping. There Murphy got off a letter to Ranger Major Jones at Austin. It began "For God's sake . . . . ."

But Murphy was more concerned with his own sake than God's. Sam surprised him in the post office and Murphy only managed to give an acceptable explanation for his presence.

On Sunday, July 14, they rode the last fourteen miles to Round Rock and camped on the San Saba road, west of Old Town. As soon as possible, Sam and Frank Jackson rode into New Town to buy feed for the horses and to reconnoiter. They returned with encouraging reports.

Seab Barnes and Murphy rode in to take a look. Barnes proposed that they steal some horses and rob the bank that night. Thoroughly alarmed, Murphy argued strongly. (He had received no word that he would be rescued soon.) Horse stealing was a heinous offense and he pointed out that if they stole horses, they would get into trouble at once. It would be better, he argued, to stay around a few days until their own mounts were rested and to pose in the meantime as cattle buyers. His arguments must have seemed valid and sensible to Barnes, because Barnes apologized to Murphy for having been suspicious of him and agreed to the plan.

Sam Bass, undoubtedly relieved that dissension had been cleared from the ranks, also agreed, and the camp was moved to a grove of live oaks, a short distance from the old cemetery. In anticipation of better times to come perhaps, a Negro woman, Mary Watson, was engaged to cook for them. Plans were made to rob the bank on the following Saturday night, when, presumably, it would have the most cash on hand.

In the meantime, back at the Ranger headquarters in Austin, Major Jones had received Murphy's letter which was posted from Georgetown, and he made ready to move. He sent a corporal to Lampasas to order the detachment of Rangers in that vicinity to proceed immediately to Round Rock. Jones sent additional men from Austin to Round Rock, headed by himself and accompanied by Deputy Sheriff Moore of Austin. He made contact too with Deputy Sheriff Grimes of Round Rock, cautioning him not to take independent action, but to cooperate with the Rangers.

A vague uneasiness and apprehension had begun to grip Sam Bass. At a distance, he saw men who looked suspiciously like Rangers to his trained eye. On Friday morning, he sent Murphy and Jackson to reconnoiter, but they reported all clear. In the late afternoon, Sam decided, since he wanted some tobacco, he would take the whole force into town and make a more careful survey. Murphy was understandably anxious to detach himself from this party, and he suggested that he detour by way of Old Town and look for Rangers there. He argued that if any were in the neighborhood, they would be there. What he actually did was seek out Deputy Grimes, describe Sam and Barnes and Jackson, and reveal their identities and their destination.

Grimes saw an opportunity to become a hero. Disregarding his instructions, he dashed off to capture the notorious trio.

Sam, Barnes and Jackson had gone to New Town, tied

their horses in an alley on the north side of the business district, and entered Henry Koppel's General Store, a rock building on the main corner, facing north.

When Deputy Grimes reached New Town, he met Deputy Moore of Austin, and asked him excitedly if he had seen three men carrying saddle bags. Moore said he had, that those three men—apparently cowboys—were in Koppel's store. He walked across the street with Grimes. Moore stopped for a few words with Koppel, who lounged outside the door while his clerk was waiting on the three strangers. The Round Rock Deputy entered the store.

There are many versions of what followed, as there were many participants and witnesses involved in the drama. The most consistent story is that Grimes walked up to the three, who were talking with the clerk. He laid his hand on Sam and demanded to know if Sam carried a pistol. All three outlaws wheeled and shot, and the ambitious deputy fell dead with six bullets in him.

A wild melee followed. Men with pistols and guns, Rangers, officials and civilians, appeared as if conjured up by an evil magician. The deputy from Austin was wounded, and the store was filled with the smoke and fumes of gunfire.

Sam met his fate in Round Rock
July the twenty first
They pierced poor Sam with rifle balls
And emptied out his purse

Sam Bass had led a charmed life. The nearest he had been to disaster had been during the North Texas chase-and-flight escapade when a stray bullet struck his gun while he held it. But Sam's luck had run out.

He and Frank Jackson got through the door with Barnes behind them. Sam's right hand had been horribly shattered and two of his fingers shot away by the fire. More men, including Major Jones, had been drawn to the scene by the firing. The three men managed to fight their way to the alley where their horses were tied. Ranger and civilians continued firing on them. Halfway down the alley, Sam was struck again by a bullet which entered his back left of the spine, tore through his kidney and exited three inches to the left side of his navel.

As they reached their horses, a Ranger sharp-shooter, shot Seab Barnes through the head, killing him instantly.

No man showed greater valor or loyalty than Frank Jackson did on this occasion. He slung Barnes' saddle bag over his right shoulder, along with his own and Sam's, and firing with the pistol in his right hand, managed to untie Sam's horse with his left and help his fatally wounded leader into the saddle. Then he untied his own horse and mounted, and, holding the bleeding, dying Sam in his saddle, they galloped off in a hail of rifle and revolver bullets.

It was nearly dark when they crossed Brushy Creek and rode toward Old Town. They failed to see Jim Murphy who hid in a feed store, but it is not likely he had failed to see them, and his feelings at the sight of his dying friend can only be imagined. When they reached their camp near the old cemetery, Frank presumably retrieved a rifle he had secreted there. Then, still holding the dying Sam in the saddle, they started in the direction of Georgetown.

Perhaps as usual, discretion was considered the better part of valor; in any case, Rangers and citizens were slow in giving chase. But when they were finally equipped and assembled, Major Jones led. They lost the trail in a cedar brake and it was decided to knock off for the time being and resume pursuit the following morning, with the arrival of the reinforcing Frontier Batallion from San Saba.

In the meantime, Sam's life blood was ebbing away in a clump of live oaks, three miles from New Town. He had become so weak that even with the aid of his loyal friend Jackson, he could ride no longer.

No one will ever know the exact parting words of the two devoted young men. It is certain that Jackson would not have left him voluntarily, and most probable that Sam told Frank he was done for, and ordered Frank to get away. Frank carefully bound Sam's wounds as best he could, tied his horse nearby, and sorrowfully left behind his friend and companion of his youth. He was never heard of again. (Fifty-eight years later, on December 24, 1936, in Williamson County, Texas, the charge against Frank Jackson of the murder of Deputy Sheriff Grimes was dismissed.)

Jim Murphy identified Barnes and the body of the young man was dumped unceremoniously into a rough wood box, and buried in an unmarked grave at the far northwest corner of the old cemetery. And that was the end of "Nubbins Colt."

For Sam Bass, it must have been a night of agony. But in the morning, he managed to crawl into an open pasture and drag himself to a farm house, but the woman there fled in terror from this bloody apparition. Others came by, but were too frightened to render any aid. He finally collapsed under a tree.

The Rangers, now reinforced and confident, picked up his trail. They passed Sam Bass in the pasture but mistook him for a railroad section hand, sleeping off a drunk. When they did meet up with a gang of railroad workers, they discovered their mistake. Returning to the pasture, Sergeant Tucker approached the prone figure warily, with pistol in hand.

"Who are you?" he asked.

"I am Sam Bass," came the reply, weakly.

Major Jones telegraphed the news of Sam's capture to Austin. The telegram was read to the State Democratic Convention, in session. One candidate promptly claimed the news was a political trick to gain favor for a candidate known to be a friend of Major Jones'.

Charges and counter charges and general excitement became so intense that the Attorney General telegraphed Major Jones to bring Sam Bass to Austin at once, if, indeed, he had captured him. The telegraph operator at Round Rock replied that the report was true, and that Major Jones had gone into the country to bring the wounded outlaw to town.

Major Jones got Dr. C.P. Cochran to ride with him and Sam was brought back in a hack, a small buggy constructed like a coach.

It was July, and naturally the weather was hot. Major Jones borrowed a hotel cot and Sam was confined in a small shack. News of what had happened brought visitors pouring into Round Rock, and Rangers were stationed both in and outside the small wooden shack, mainly for the purpose of keeping visitors out.

The Doctor examined Sam carefully and stated he could live for only a very short time. He dressed the wounds and stayed with his patient constantly. Cochran's bill, presumably presented to the state, read:

July 23, 1878

For medical services rendered Sam Bass whilst a state prisoner near Round Rock, Texas.

Visit and dressing wounds	$10.00
Detention for 36 hours	30.00
Total	$40.00

A Negro nurse was hired for the suffering and rapidly failing prisoner. Food was brought, but Sam was too weak and badly wounded to eat. Nevertheless, he was subjected to relentless questioning by Major Jones and others. They learned nothing from him. The substance of his replies are as follows:

"It is not in my profession to tell what I know. It is agin my profession to blow on pals. If a man knows anything like that about friends it ought to die in him. About the shooting in Koppel's store, Grimes asked me if I had a pistol. I said I had and then all three of us drew and shot. If I killed Grimes, he was the first man I ever killed and it had to be him or me."

The **Galveston News,** then the leading newspaper in Texas, sent a special writer to the scene and he was permitted to interview Sam. The reporter was more gentle with the dying young man than the others had been, and he got additional information. By then, of course, Sam knew that Barnes was dead, that Jackson had escaped and that Murphy had betrayed them all. Stating his age incorrectly—perhaps intentionally—Sam gave a statement with full knowledge that death was near:

> "Yes, I'm Sam Bass. I'm shot to pieces and there's no use to deny it. I'm twenty-five years old and I have four brothers and two sisters. I don't know anyone in Round Rock. I intended to make a raid on a bank here and go on to Mexico. There were four of us. Three men that meant business—and one drag."

Asked how he began his violent and lawless life, Sam said:

> "I started out sporting on horses. I got worse when they robbed me of my first three hundred dollars. Then I went to robbing stages up in the Black Hills. Yes, Collins and I robbed the U.P. I don't know if it did either of us much good. There's no use to talk about religion. It's too late. And I know I'm going to hell anyhow."

He spent another dreadful night in the suffocating hot

wood shack, with only curious and unfriendly eyes upon him. His physical strength, resulting from an active, outdoor life, served only to prolong the agony. By Sunday noon he was much worse. Nevertheless, Ranger inquisitors again subjected him to questioning.

In mid-afternoon, the doctor told him he was dying and asked if he wished to make any statement.

"Just let me go," said Sam wearily.

A few minutes later, he said to his nurse, "The world is bobbin' around."

He died at 3:58 P.M. on July 21, 1878 his twenty-seventh birthday.

Jim Murphy talked for hours with newspapermen. He gave a detailed story of the gang's last trip, and of the dangers he had personally undergone. He fancied that he would achieve the status of a great public benefactor.

And so he sold out Sam and Barnes
And left their friends to mourn
Oh, what a scorching Jim will get
When Gabriel blows his horn!

Instead of receiving praise and attention, Jim Murphy became known as the "Spy Hero." But the Rangers kept their bargain, and Murphy returned to Denton a free man.

Perhaps he got to Heaven
There's none of us can say
But if I'm right in my surmise
He's gone the other way

Spurned by all, and overcome with remorse, Jim Murphy committed suicide less than a year later on June 9, 1879. Poison was taken by accident or intent.

> But the man who plays the traitor
> Will feel it bye and bye
> His death was so uncommon
> 'T'was poison in the eye

A number of people gathered to hold a wake for Sam Bass, and a Round Rock cabinet maker worked all night to fashion a respectable coffin. On Monday morning, six paid black pallbearers loaded the coffin holding his mortal remains into a wagon. The State made final disposition of the dead outlaw, without fuss or furbelows. But as the procession wended its way from New Town across Brushy Creek and into Old Town, it grew by hundreds. Reverend J.W. Ledbetter, the Methodist minister, joined it as it passed his house.

Sam Bass was buried alongside the new grave of Seab Barnes in the far corner of the cemetery. The clergyman made a few appropriate remarks, and offered a prayer.

> Poor Sam he is a corpse now
> And six feet under clay
> And Jackson's in the bushes
> Trying to get away

In September of 1879, Mrs. Sally Bass Hornbrook visited her brother's grave and had a monument erected. It was of pink marble and consisted of a base surmounted by a shaft. On it beside the name and dates, were these words:

> "A brave man reposes in death here.
> Why was he not true?"

Within a few years, the pink marble monument had disappeared completely, literally chipped off and carried away by swarms of indefatigable souvenir hunters. A second and a third monument, and even a marker for the grave of Seab Barnes met similar fate.

In 1923, approximately, R.E. Loving, the Round Rock monument dealer, put small concrete slabs on each of the graves, but these, too, vanished, either by disintegration or otherwise. Until the placement of the last monument by the citizens of Round Rock, paid for by contributions from passing visitors, there was only a head stone and foot stone of very soft limestome. Bits taken from it would very likely have crumbled into dust immediately, and if there ever had been any carving or inscription on either of those stones, it had eroded long ago.

The bright new polished granite marker was placed, somewhat unusually, in the center of the grave between the old crumbled markers. And now, new generations of visitors may come to see the grave of Sam Bass, suitably and decently marked.

Now you have heard the story
Of Sam Bass, good and bad,
And I'll allow as you will
"T'was mighty, mighty, sad."

SAM BASS grave stone in Round Rock, Texas cemetery.

PART 4

Belle Starr

BELLE STARR AND BLUE DUCK

BELLE STARR
1848—1889

Scyene Road is an important thoroughfare in Dallas, a few blocks south of the Dallas Fair Park with its famous Cotton Bowl. Most of the citizens of Dallas have been on Scyene Road at some time or other, but when asked the derivation or the significance of the name, many, if not most, would have to confess ignorance. Scyene—or what was once Scyene—now an integral part of the city, used to be a small settlement, six miles east of Dallas, and more than one hundred years ago it was the home of the most sensational and energetic woman who ever dazzled and bemused the "cafe society" in the city.

Myra Belle Shirley was the name the woman was given: a woman completely amoral, totally uninhibited, more sexually adventurous than the average man. As long as her looks lasted, she exercised her feminine wiles and physical charms, but even before the inevitable erosion of the years had wasted these, she wore two delicately fashioned, but very lethal, revolvers, with pearl handles and silver filigree, and these were not merely for ornamentation.

Belle Starr became a celebrity early in life, and after her death the image extended and grew. It was a tribute to her fame that while the "dime novel" which dealt with such as Sam Bass, Jesse James or Cole Younger, sold indeed for a dime, those "dime novels" which were about her sold for twenty-five cents, notably the book published by Richard Fox of the National Police Gazette, a book as entertaining as it was unreliable.

BELLE STARR'S grave and cabin at Younger's Bend.

She was also the heroine or central figure in a number of motion pictures which were all given the careless Hollywood treatment, and there were several melodramas that featured her story. However, the fact is that so many of the tales told about her were spurious, yet some of the most improbable was true. "Liberated" she was, in her fashion.

As generally acknowledged by valid historians, the best of all the Belle Starr books was by Burton Rascoe in 1941. It had a title to end all titles: "Belle Starr, The Bandit Queen, The True Story of the Romantic and Exciting Career of the Daring and Glamorous Lady Famed in Legend and Story throughout the West As the Beautiful Girl Who Would never have Went Wrong if Things Hadn't Gone Wrong. The true Facts about the Dastardly Deeds and The Come-Uppence of Such Dick Turpins, Robin Hoods and Rini Rinaldos as The Youngers, the Jameses, the Daltons, the Starrs, the Doolins and the Jenningses. The Real Story with Court Records and Contemporary Newspaper Accounts and Testimony of Old Nesters, here and there, in the Southwest. A Veritable Exposee of Badmen and Marshals and Why Crime Does Not Pay!" No author or publisher ever held tongue in cheek longer than that.

Myra Belle Shirley was born on a farm near Shirley, Missouri, on February 5, 1848. (Shirley is now a town on State Highway 8, some seventy-two miles east of St. Louis.) Her parents were John and Elizabeth Shirley, and she was preceded by two brothers: Preston ("Shug" for "Sugar"), aged twelve, and Ed, aged ten.

The Shirleys were people of some consequence in the community, as evidenced by the town's name, and her father was a reasonably successful farmer and trader. When Myra Belle was eight years old, the family moved to Carthage, the county seat of Jasper County. The principal reason for the move was to improve their financial opportunities and to obtain better schooling facilities for the children.

Carthage was on the Captain Marcy Trail, the direct outlet to the great Southwset, and to golden California. Mr. Shirley already owned land in the vicinity, and he sold it to open a hotel on the square in Carthage. It occupied an entire block, and included a livery stable, blacksmith shop, and other related businesses which served the travelling public. He also owned several slaves.

The younger Shirleys entered the William Craven Private School in Carthage, and Myra Belle, presumably after completing preparatory courses, was enrolled in the fashionable Carthage Female Academy. This "finishing school" specialized in teaching drawing room arts and lady-like deportment, which would complete the polishing of a perfect young gentlewoman.

A schoolmate recalled that Myra Belle was a "nice little girl . . . in fact, the entire Shirley family were nice people."

Their pleasant and prosperous life was to be short-lived. Abolitionist violence was beginning in Kansas and Missouri. Like that ancient Carthage, their Carthage was destroyed. In 1862, it was burned to the ground, with only the court house left standing. Ed Shirley had been killed in a guerilla raid and Preston, "Shug" Shirley had gone.

John and Elizabeth Shirley, with their daughter, Myra Belle, packed up what was left and set out by wagon for Texas, hoping to reunite there with Preston.

Compared to Carthage, Dallas, Texas was a growing metropolis. The Shirleys found Preston living in Scyene, a small, wooded settlement between Dallas and Mesquite, and moved in with him.

Myra Belle, or Belle as we will call her from this point, was a tender sixteen. She had a nice figure, of average size, a light complexion, and dark hair and eyes. She was entered at once in Mrs. Poole's Community School.

A nearby and well-to-do neighbor was Elder Amos McCommas, and he had a daughter named Rosa who was about the same age as Belle. The Shirleys were strangers to the community, of course; they had no connections or introductions, no wealth nor servants. Belle tried to make friends with Rosa McCommas, but was brutally snubbed. Belle never forgave or forgot, and would take amusing revenge a few years later.

The largest house in the settlement was that of Colonel Younger's sons, and it was capably presided over by a sister. John and Bob Younger sang in the church choir and Jim Younger even became a deputy sheriff. But the Youngers lived more or less in seclusion, which became more pronounced with the arrival of another brother, named Cole, who was accompanied by a friend named Jesse James.

The visit of Cole Younger and Jesse James was a vacation of sorts, and they preferred to remain incognito. Belle Shirley and Cole Younger met. He was young and good-looking: five feet eleven inches tall, with brown hair, blue eyes, and a convincing conversational flair. They fell in love, but since Cole could not appear publicly, their meetings were clandestine and the results were predictable.

The summer idyll came to an abrupt end when Cole, perhaps in the nature of his profession, received an urgent summons and took "French leave," without leaving a forwarding address. One can be forgiven the suspicion, perhaps, that his abrupt departure had something to do with the fact that Belle was pregnant. In the parlance of the day, "ruined and disgraced."

The distress of the Shirley family can be easily understood, but it was assuaged by Belle's assurances that she and Cole Younger were married. Marriages in pioneer America were not matters requiring license and public recording; the English Common Law recognized the legality of much less ceremonimus unions. Belle's parents accepted her explanation that she had been married by an itinerant preacher.

In due time, her baby was born; it was a girl, and she named it Pearl.

As a mother, Belle no longer felt the necessity for consulting her parents about her activities. She got a job as an entertainer in a Dallas saloon and dance-hall, and put on highly "lady-like" song-and-dance acts, and she was an outstanding hit. Such a success, in fact, that she progressed to the position of hostess and lady-gambler, alternating as the only woman card dealer at faro and poker.

She became famous in Dallas society, and a favorite of the class which had hitherto neglected her.

She dressed in the high fashion of the day: tightly laced velvets, revealing a tantalizing cleavage which suggested in turn additional feminine charms.

Cole Younger returned to Dallas and after witnessing the glamorous transformation, suggested they resume their relationship. Belle, in view of his long and unexplained absence, refused, and Cole left at once.

Mr. and Mrs. Shirley became seriously concerned with their daughter's conduct. On one of her visits to them, they forcibly restrained her. A few days later, a group of her friends stormed the house and rescued her. After some weeks, the worried parents received a letter in which she advised them she had married Jim Reed, an old Carthage friend, and that he had taken her back to Missouri.

The wedding must have been a colorful affair, with all participants on horseback, and the ceremony performed by a small-time Texas stage coach robber who posed as an itinerant preacher. The "preacher", John Fisher, had presided at the "marriage" of Belle and Cole Younger.

Jim Reed was an Indian, six feet six inches tall, and it was said that he could break a gun barrel across his knee as easily as the average man could snap a broomstick. He was a thief and outlaw, and a true son of his notorious father, Thomas Reed.

At Rich Hill, Missouri, where the couple took up residence, Jim and Belle had many friends, and one evening,

Jim brought home for dinner a handsome young Indian named Sam Starr. He and Belle were mutually attracted, but at the time nothing came of it.

Jim Reed had urgent business at hand. His brother had been shot by the "Shannon boys." Although it was admitted that the shooting was accidental and a case of mistaken identity, the explanation did not satisfy Jim Reed. He killed both the Shannons and afterward Belle wrote home that Jim was taking her and little Pearl to California, "in order to get away from the hot weather." It was very hot in Missouri for Jim Reed: there was a price on his head. They stayed in California for two years, during which time Belle presented her husband with a son, whom they named Ed. (Some accounts claim that Jim Reed was the father of both Pearl and Ed, but Belle steadfastly maintained that Pearl was Cole Younger's daughter, and she, of all persons, should have known.)

It was to Oklahoma that Belle and Jim Reed returned. Here Belle planned and carried out her first big job. She did it alone.

An old Creek Indian, named Watt Grayson, lived near Eufaula. He was a hermit and miser, and was rumored to have large sums of money hidden in or near his home. Newspaper reports claimed that Belle tortured the aged recluse until he revealed the hiding place of the cache, and that she made off with it. This, Belle indignantly denied. She said that all she did was to place a noose around the old Indian's neck, throw the rope over a convenient rafter, and playfully pull him up and down a few times until he reached a cooperative frame of mind. Belle took $20,000, judiciously rejecting $12,000 in Confederate currency.

Belle and Jim Reed returned to Dallas, and Belle's parents received them kindly. They had become more reconciled to the actions of the younger generation, especially after Belle financed a small hotel for her father.

Dallas received its favorite with open arms. Belle took a

suite at the fashionable Planters Hotel. With these stylish quarters, she also maintained a bevy of servants, several fine carriages, and high-stepping horses. For riding, her favorite horse was a black, star-blazed stallion. Riding side-saddle, wearing a white Stetson hat decorated with flowing ostrich plumes, a white chiffon blouse, voluminous black velvet skirts, and embroidered high boots, she must have been wondrous to behold.

Whatever her costume, she invariably wore a beautiful silver cartridge belt, and on each side of it hung a dainty revolver with mother-of-pearl handles. It was said that she occasionally masqueraded in men's clothing in order to mix with the boys and find out what was going on in the world.

Jim was a bargainer and a horse trader; he travelled frequently and Belle occasionally went on trips with him. They were in South Texas, on the San Marcos River, in a crowd of picnickers and Jim was making a horse trade, when Belle settled an old score. The horsetrading was an entertainment in itself. When he had made a deal and had received what he knew to be the last dollar from the buyer, Jim Reed offered to "throw in" his "girlfriend," for an extra twenty-five dollars. The girlfriend, Belle, said that her name was Rosa McCommas, of Scyene, Texas; this being, of course, the name of the girl who had so badly snubbed Belle.

The story gained wide circulation, aided beyond doubt by Belle's efforts in the hope it all would reach the ears of Miss McCommas.

This story and others have been skeptically viewed, but when stories pass permanently into folklore, rejections are of no avail. Numerous tales like this one were related in a book which appeared after her death, entitled "Belle Starr, The Bandit Queen, or The Female Jesse James." It was a best-seller in its day, but now is seen rarely if ever, except in the collections of such literature.

Jim Reed's principal business venture in south Texas

was robbing the Austin-San Antonio stagecoach, on April 7, 1874. The road on which this occurred had come to be known as the Post Road. At the time of the robbery, the stage carried the United States mail and $2,500 in currency. In addition, there were a number of prominent passengers, including a Methodist Bishop. The robbers took the money, ripped open all the mail bags and took one of the bags away with them.

The United States Government and the Governor of Texas each offered rewards of $3,000 for the apprehension of the robbers, and the stage coach company added another $1,000 in reward money. Robbing the mail was a serious offense, and the fact that it had been done in a populous section of the state only added to the seriousness, so far as authorities were concerned.

Reed and his assistants were positively identified as the men who had performed the robbery, and soon thereafter, Reed was shot and killed near Paris, Texas while resisting arrest.

Belle went into immediate retirement. In her widowhood, she centered her time and attention on her daughter Pearl. Belle well-remembered her own musical instruction at Carthage Female Academy in Missouri, and her own successful stage experience, and it is not misstating the case to say she envisioned a glorious career for Pearl. She trained her daughter in singing and dancing, and the theatrical arts in general.

Talent agents and theatrical entrepreneurs have always fled from the determined mother who has in tow an embryonic child-star. Such action would have been foolhardy or ineffective in dealing with a mother who carried a couple of revolvers and who was known to be a crackshot. Pearl made her theatrical debut at the age of fourteen.

However, she soon "retired" as the result of illness and because she did not like vaudeville life. Somehow theater in Dallas managed to survive, and so did Belle's ebulliency.

A story relates that on an afternoon ride with a friend named Emma Jones, Belle passed the store in a small settlement nearby. The owner of the store was much disliked. Emma Jones, in an effort to show off for her adventurous companion, attempted to set fire to the store. When she proved inept at the business, Belle showed her how it should be done, and in a burst of jealousy, Emma Jones reported her to the law. Belle was arrested and tried for arson. The trial was the prime topic in Dallas and a wealthy rancher, named Patterson, who was visiting Dallas at the time, dropped in at the court house to see and hear more. He was so moved by the spectacle of Belle in distress that he stepped forth and paid all damages and costs for her, and even pressed a sum of money upon Pearl, as compensation for her inconvenience and mental suffering.

In an interview, Belle admitted two intense dislikes: women and newspaper reporters. In view of the snub by Rosa McCommas and the treachery of Emma Jones, the former feeling is at least understandable. But as for the reporter prejudice, it is a matter of timing. Belle was, we might say, like an artist who dislikes being watched as he mixes his paints and applies them to canvas, but still wishes all the world to see and admire the masterpiece when it is completed. Belle did not want reporters snooping around as she worked her schemes, but when she had pulled off some daring effect, she enjoyed flattering publicity. She wrote often to newspapers, and her letters dealt exclusively with Belle Starr, (or Belle Reed as she was then known). They were lengthy and couched in flowery terms. More sophisticated reporters wrote of her with mocking grandiloquence, and she took it quite seriously.

After the happy conclusion to the arson episode, she had a spot of trouble with a complaint of horse stealing. On that occasion, she was actually placed in jail. Shortly after her lock-up, she disappeared with the turnkey. Within a few days, the embarrassed turnkey returned bearing a note for the sheriff from Belle, in which she had written that she found the turnkey "unsatisfactory for any purpose whatsoever."

The victim claimed he had been forced to leave with his prisoner at gunpoint, to accompany her to a hideout, to do the most menial labor for her. He had providentially escaped, found the letter to the sheriff in his pocket, and decided it ought to be delivered. The horse stealing charge against Belle was dismissed, and the turnkey's pistol was returned to him, it is said, decorated with a big yellow ribbon bow.

Belle departed for Oklahoma, shaking from her feet forever the dust of Dallas. It is conjectured that the primary reason she did so was news that Cole Younger was in the penitentiary at Stillwater, Oklahoma and that Belle wished to be as near him as possible. Although she had no immediate plans to continue the program to make a lady of Pearl, she now became actively concerned in her abiding passion to free Cole Younger.

This energetic, preposterous woman was intelligent enough to realize that money—a great deal of it—would be necessary, and from this time, in her pursuit of cash, all protense of respectability was dropped for good.

She robbed any number of banks, but in an unspectacular manner and with scant yields, compared to others of the time. (Part of her love for Cole Younger was recognition of his prowess and finesse in such undertakings.) She had a peculiar but reasonably successful technique, in which she was decoy rather than principal. She would enter a small bank at noon, when only one or two men were on duty. There she would engage their attention under some pretext of business, feigning feminine helplessness in such matters. At a pre-arranged time or signal, her confederate would enter. Sometimes the cash drawers could be emptied before the bankers knew what had happened; at other times they would be enticed away from the money and their own protective pistols, so that the robberies were accomplished noiselessly and efficiently. The pretty young woman would disappear in the excitement which followed and was seldom suspected of complicity. It is a matter of speculation where the money went, but she was said to have been scrupulously prompt and honest in dealing with tradesmen and suppliers for her own purposes.

Belle's attachment for her late husband and for Cole Younger did not preclude other practical and romantic attachments. Her next "husband," or protector, was a man with the intriguing name of "Blue Duck." Their first act together was rounding up a herd of cattle and selling it to an unsuspecting purchaser for $7,000. (In livestock deals, the doctrine of **caveat emptor**—Let the buyer beware—has prevailed to the present day.)

Afterward, while Belle was relaxing in Dodge City, Kansas, she received word that Blue Duck was losing his shirt and the money in a crooked gambling game down the street. Dressing hastily, but not forgetting her pistols, she entered the gambling hall just as the last bill was passing across the table. Belle seethed. Holding a pistol with one hand she scooped up the seven thousand with the other—taking a little extra for her time and trouble—and then, shielding Blue Duck, she backed out of the place, cursing the gamblers. They did nothing to retaliate, and must have dismissed the event as a woman's tantrum.

Blue Duck seems to have been more protected than protecting. A photograph exists of him and Belle. In the picture, Blue Duck, with his weak-looking but handsome face, with its carefully trimmed small mustache, reclines on an ornate sofa while Belle stands, behind and above him, watchful and confident, but dour and unattractively stocky. Her protective interest in him endured, and when later he was tried for murder, she not only appeared as a witness in his behalf, but employed an expensive lawyer who obtained an unusually light sentence of life imprisonment for him, rather than the customary hanging. Later, Belle succeeded in getting Blue Duck pardoned. It was a waste of money, as it turned out, for Blue Duck was murdered soon after that by an unknown party. He was succeeded in Belle's affections by a man named Jack Spaniard, who was hung for murder. Belle took as his successor one Jim French, who died by violence while committing a burglary.

Belle was getting on in years, as the phrase has it, but there was no diminishing of energy. She remembered the attractive Sam Starr, whom Jim Reed had one evening brought home to share their dinner. She sought him out and married him.

This was not such a simple process. Sam Starr was an Indian and all Indians had, by law, become wards of the United States government, which was alloting land, cattle, and other forms of relief to the members of the Five Civilized Tribes.

Sam Starr received some land which was ideally suited to the purposes that Belle had in mind. Although it was, to say the least, alien to Belle's character to consult Uncle Sam as a guardian on matters concerning her and Sam Starr's welfare, she had to possess the required legal status in order to live on his land and, in view of her record, she was viewed with repugnance and suspicion by the benign Guardian. The Government was also trying to make restitution for its own past sins and delinquencies, one of which was its failure to have protected the old Creek Indian, Watt Grayson, from the robbery of his $20,000. Criminal action against Belle could not be taken without a suitable witness to his having possessed the money and to his having been robbed of it.

In order to further her plan to marry Sam Starr, and as evidence of good faith, Belle made a treaty with the Creek Nation, in which she made restitution—a matter of simply robbing Peter to pay Paul. But in so making a treaty, however insignificant it may have been, she achieved the status of queen and potentate. And when she became the legal wife of Sam Starr, she automatically became a citizen of the Cherokee Nation, which status carried with it many immunities and privileges. She also acquired the name by which forever afterward she would be known—Belle Starr. "Beautiful Star." She could properly have been called a Shooting Star, but in fairness it must be noted that while she committed nearly every crime from arson to bootlegging, through an entire alphabet, she is never known to have killed anyone, although she may well have been an accomplice to such acts.

The land Sam Starr owned was on a bank of the Canadian River near the little town of Eufaula, Oklahoma. With fond remembrance of her first love, Belle named it Younger's Bend.

If today you should wish to visit Younger's Bend, where nothing remains but the meager ruins of Belle's tomb, you would find it difficult to reach. Then, however, it was as impregnable as if protected by moat and drawbridge. The entrance was through a narrow canyon.

Belle's statement was "No man enters Younger's Bend without first giving a thorough account of himself before he gets out." While the phraseology is somewhat involved, the meaning is clear. It was true that no visitor could gain entrance without having been observed in time to make suitable arrangements for his reception.

On a high bluff rising steeply from the river, she built the main house. (Later, the heights became known as "Belle's Butte," but vulgar neighbors called it "Belle's Butt," which, indeed, had grown ample with time and easy living.) She also built a number of smaller guest houses.

In order to put the place on a self-sustaining, or paying basis, it was Belle's plan to operate a type of retreat where paying guests, gentlemen only, could rest in seclusion and anonymity. One of the first of these paying guests was "Mr. Williams, an old friend from Texas." "Mr. Williams" died some years later. He had mounted a chair at his home in Missouri, (where he lived under the name of "Mr. Howard") in order to straighten the picture hanging on the wall of his favorite race horse, "Skyrocket." His carelessness was fatal. He had neglected to lower the window shade and had laid his pistol on the bed before mounting the chair. Thus, with his back turned, he offered an easy and tempting target for Bob Ford, trusted associate, to whom the Governor of the state had offered ten thousand dollars reward for Mr. Howard, dead or alive. Ford shot Mr. Howard cleanly through the head. Mr. Howard fell dead. Jesse James was dead.

For additional income, Belle went into the beverage business. She distilled a popular brew. Although it is said that she produced "good stuff," it was illegal for anyone to make, possess, sell, buy, or drink anything of an intoxicating nature, good or bad, in the Indian Territories. Belle and her distributors had trouble.

She was, as has been mentioned, an indefatigable letter writer, and she once gave out a statement reflecting her hurt and injury:

"Far from society, I settled permanently on a place of picturesque beauty on the Canadian River. There I hoped to pass the rest of my life in peace and quietude with my handsome husband, Sam Starr, a Cherokee Indian, who was a son of the noted Tom Starr, with my beautiful daughter, Pearl Younger, 'the Canadian Rose' and my son, Ed Reed—children of previous marriages."

(Tom Starr was noted alright, having been one of the most dangerous criminals in the territories.)

"But slanderous gossip by shoddy whites who are living in the Indian Territory solely for the purpose of evading payments of taxes on their dogs, made my home famous as an outlaw's ranch, long before any of the boys visited me. I never wrote to any of my old associates, and I wished them to know nothing of my whereabouts. Through rumor they found out about it."

A widely circulated Texas newspaper printed a revision and extension of Belle's statement later. In it, she complains that she was being charged with every depredation and robbery that took place in the Indian Territory. She said that she was the best guarded woman in the country, that if a United States Marshal was not watching her, a deputy was. And she reaffirmed—using the news story as an advertisement of sorts—that she was a friend to "any brave, gallant outlaw" in need of rest or reformation and that, as a matter of fact, the welcome mat was out at the moment for three or four "jolly fellows" whose present whereabouts were unknown but "of great interest to certain parties."

The very plain truth was that Belle Starr, during these years, was operating a hide-away for criminals, and was master-minding a dangerous gang of thieves and cutthroats. The wide open towns of Catoosa, Claremore, and Tulsa were not far distant and afforded convenient connections for the disposal of stolen property. (In the territories, possession of anything was considerably more than a mere nine-tenths of the law.)

Belle, need we add, was no recluse. She was often in the bars and saloons, drinking, gambling, and shooting. At times she would play the piano and sing, exuberantly or sadly, as mood dictated. Among the illiterate outlaws, her education seemed fantastic; she even read books for entertainment and information.

Large sums of money went through her hands and much of was spent to obtain special privileges and dispensations for Cole Younger, as well as to keep alive the efforts to secure his pardon or parole. Frequently, she was seen in Fort Smith, Arkansas, and other larger towns, and her missions to these places were usually to obtain dismissal of charges and complaints against her friends and associates, or guests. She never hesitated in employing able and expensive lawyers, and she had remarkable success in aiding her comrades. Nearly always with her, and on display, were one or more of the fine revolvers which she claimed were the only things in the world more beautiful than fine horses.

It seems odd that although complaints and indictments against her were innumerable, the only charge for which she was ever actually tried and convicted was a comparatively minor one by modern standards—stealing two horses. She and Sam were both arrested and they quickly made bond at Ft. Smith. A number of peculiar circumstances characterized the trial that led to her conviction.

The spectacular "Bandit Queen" was arraigned before an equally spectacular jurist. He was "Hanging Judge Parker," and this amazing person presided over an equally amazing court for twenty-one years. It was a United States District Court. It was both a Federal District Court, and an Appeals Court, and also the Supreme Court, as far as his decisions were concerned. Its record and jurisdiction made it one of the most extraordinary phenomena in the history of American jurisprudence. For fourteen years, there was no appeal possible to a higher court from Parker's decisions—at least it took that long for the government to get around to curtailing his authority. For the last seven years of his rule, before he died of chagrain and other causes, appeals could be taken.

During his tenure of office, he tried over 13,000 cases, which is an average of more than one per day including Sundays and holidays. He found 9,454 defendants guilty. He sentenced 172 men to "death by hanging" and 88 of these sentences were carried out. More would have been, but 84 of his convictions were reversed or modified on appeal after his decisions ceased to be final. The records of his court have been preserved in a Federal Archives Building at Ft. Worth.

The combination of Belle Starr and Judge Parker was bound to be a dazzling attraction of the most sensational sort. Before the trial, she had already gained national notoriety, but the publicity which attended this proceeding was to elevate her into the top ranks of national and international celebrities. The telegraph, that comparatively new marvel, was available at Ft. Smith and star reporters from the great newspapers descended in droves on the city. Belle and Sam had the best counsel available, and it was observed that these experienced lawyers paid close attention to all suggestions Belle made during the trial's progress.

A Ft. Smith newspaper recorded: "the very idea of a woman being charged with an offense of this kind and the fact that she was queen and guiding spirit of an outlaw band was sufficient to fill the court room."

The defendents were found guilty. The visiting special writers sent out reams of copy. After all, as one gallant commenter reflected, Belle was convicted jointly with her husband, and it was but natural that a loving wife should share the trials and vicissitudes of her husband's life.

Belle wrote a touching good-bye letter to "Baby Pearl," but she and Sam were back home in a little less than nine months. The "Queen" resumed her throne, and in May, 1885, Belle and the Judge demonstrated that no rancor existed between them, when they participated in a "Wild West" production for the County Fair at Little Rock, Arkansas.

The top attraction was a dramatic enactment of a stage coach robbery. The performers were real stars and were paid accordingly. Difficult though it may be to believe, Judge Parker rode as a passenger in the stagecoach and the coach was held up by none other than Belle Starr, the Bandit Queen. Belle needed little or no rehearsal. Her pistols, however, at the request of the Judge, were carefully examined before each performance to be certain that all the cartridges were blanks. The star performers received exorbitant fees, and every show was sold out.

The Belle Starr of this period has been variously described by newspaper reporters.

"Belle attracts considerable attention wherever she goes, being a dashing horsewoman and exceedingly graceful in the saddle. She dresses plainly and wears a broad-brimmed, white, man's hat, surmounted by a wide, black plush band with feathers and ornaments which is very becoming to her . . . She is of medium size, well-formed, a dark brunette with bright, intelligent, black eyes . . . Belle is a crack shot and handles her pistols with as much dexterity as any frontiersman . . . a reckless, daring expression . . . as an equestrienne, Belle Starr is without a rival . . . Her appearance is of that kind as would be sure to attract the attention of wild and desperate men."

A photograph taken of her a short time before her death shows a plump, coarse, dark woman with forbidding countenance.

All of Belle's husbands were travelling men, likely to be away from home very often. During one long trip of Sam Starr's, she received as paying guest, young and handsome John Middleton, a cousin of the late Jim Reed. Middleton was wanted in various places for an assortment of crimes. With Belle, acquaintance turned to friendship and friendship ripened into love. At length, expecting the imminent return of Sam Starr, the two decided to elope. It was decided very wisely that they should take different routes to a distant rendezvous. Belle arrived at the meeting place and waited in vain. John Middleton never made it. His body was found on the bank of a creek, badly decomposed or eaten by animals. But it was plain he had been shot, and the supposition was that Sam Starr had pulled a shotgun's trigger in defense of his home. Middleton was buried in a pauper's grave, and when Belle was so informed, she had the body disinterred and given decent burial, complete with marker.

Sam and Belle effected a reconciliation and returned to a more or less happy domestic life at Younger's Bend. Tranquility was not to last for long. Belle was arrested for complicity with Sam Starr in the theft of the horse which had belonged to John Middleton, which he had been riding when he was killed. The consensus, apparently, was that John Middleton had got what was coming to him, regardless of who had done it, but stealing a horse was a serious offense. Belle and Sam had been convicted of a similar theft and this new charge called for prompt and decisive action by the authorities. To add to the seriousness, Sam was also wanted on a variety of other charges, including one by the Creek Nation for robbing its treasury; for postal theft, by the U.S. Marshals; for burglary and numerous other offenses. Belle realized that Federal punishment would be much milder than the retributive justice customary in the Indian tribal laws, and she persuaded Sam Starr to go with her to Ft. Smith and surrender to the authorities there. She had no difficulty then in getting the charge against herself dismissed, but getting Sam out of the trouble was a longer and more involved problem. However, with her usual efficiency, she got him released on bond.

And while at liberty, Sam Starr met up with Frank West. The Starr and West families were related, but were on bad terms and none can be such bitter enemies as estranged relatives. One of the Wests had given the testimony in court which had sent Belle and Sam to the penitentiary for horse stealing. The meeting of Sam Starr and Frank West was a furious gun battle. Both were expert shots. They killed each other at the same moment.

The widow Belle Starr grieved for her husband with suitable display, but soon found solace in Jim July, a tall, dark and handsome young Indian with glistening, black, shoulder-length hair. As Belle grew progressively older, she selected younger partners. There is a general tendency among us to believe that although time deals harshly with friends and acquaintances, it is more indulgent with oneself.

Belle was nearing a middle-aged forty, and Jim July had just reached the age of twenty-four. Belle did not intend to become another page in the old story of July married to December, and, besides, she liked the melodious sound of "Belle Starr." As the legal widow of Sam Starr she was now sole owner of Younger's Bend. Furthermore, Pearl was approaching womanhood and if she were to maintain the special position Belle envisioned for her, there had to be an aura of some respectability. The solution was both simple and practical to one with Belle's resourceful mind: she advised Jim July that he would have to drop his own last name and adopt the surname of Starr; otherwise, he would be subjected to the contempt and disgrace of being known simply as "Belle Starr's husband." Jim chose to live in dignity, and became Jim Starr. Yet, even with all this satisfactorily adjusted, heart-break soon came.

"Baby Pearl," "The Candian Rose," became pregnant. In her dark suspicions, Belle even cast a speculative eye on tall, dark Jim July Starr. Pearl, however, admitted frankly that she could not be positive as to the identity of her misfortune's author.

Belle took Pearl to Ft. Smith and arranged a hasty marriage with a vagrant, foot-loose bucko, immediately afterward issuing him his discharge papers, travel orders, suitable pay and expense money. Pearl, with every possible attention, had her baby at Siloam Springs, Arkansas. It was a girl and was given the name Flossie. Belle Starr never even looked at the infant, fearing possibly that some resemblance she saw would raise suspicions. She had the infant put out for adoption two days after it was born. Pearl, forgiven, came home with her mother.

Later in the same year, the Honorable Robert L. Owen, United States Indian Agent, and later U.S. Senator, wrote an open letter to Belle Starr and had it published in the newspapers. It began:

"The complaint against you for harboring bad characters has not, in my opinion, been established and is now dismissed."

It might be thought that with exoneration by so distinguished a figure, Belle Starr would have turned over a new leaf and became a useful member of society. This would be a pleasant assumption, but it is more probable that the effect of this statement was to give her additional contempt for the law. Actually, her way of life changed very little. It is certain that the absolution by the Hon. Mr. Owen had no salutary effect on Jim July Starr. Some bothersome charges had been filed against him and Belle thought it best for him to go to Ft. Smith and make the necessary explanations in person.

It was February and there had been a refreshing rain; the weather was pleasant and bracing. Belle decided that she would ride part of the way with her husband, expecting to return home by nightfall. Her comings and goings were unpredictable, and Pearl felt no alarm when her mother did not return home that night. But when the riderless horse, laden with fancily decorated bridle and silver-mounted saddle, came in the following day, an alarm was given and a search instituted.

Belle Starr was found dead, face down in the mud, riddled with buckshot. She had been shot in the back and undoubtedly by a man. The age of chivalry was dead in Oklahoma, along with Belle Starr, "The Terror of the Territories."

A neighboring farmer, Edgar Watson, was accused of her murder. (Belle was said to have gathered some scandalous information about him and hinted to him that it was for sale.) But Watson was cleared.

There was strong suspicion about Jim July Starr, too. On the day preceding Belle's death, he had borrowed a double-barrelled shotgun, of the identical type used, from Watson, and his reason for having borrowed it, he declared, was that he wanted to shoot "some wolves." The real murderer was never apprehended. Many years later, however, a story was circulated about a delayed confession supposedly made by Jim Middleton, brother of John

Middleton, Belle's short-term lover. Jim Middleton, so the story goes, made the admission with one eye on the protection of the statute of limitations and the other on the impossibility of any admissible evidence against him. His statement was that his brother, John, always carried five thousand dollars in his saddlebags, and that he, Jim, had known that Belle, alone or in conjunction with Sam Starr, had killed John Middleton and taken the money. He claimed his motive was revenge, though it had taken him several years to get around to killing Belle, but he never said whether it was revenge for the murder of his brother or for the appropriation of the sum he alleged his brother had carried.

In a very real sense, Belle Starr was a **femme fatale**. Except for Cole Younger, each of her lovers died a violent death. Cole lived longest, no doubt because he was in the safest and most secure place—jail. Jim July Starr did not survive her even a year. He was shot and killed.

Below is listed the chronology:

Jim Reed .... shot by officers August 6, 1874
John Middleton .... killed May 1885
Blue Duck .... killed July 1886
Sam Starr .... killed December 1886
Jack Spaniard .... killed August 1889
Jim French .... killed while committing burglary
                                    exact date not known
Jim July Starr................ killed January 1890

Belle was two days less than forty-one years old at the time of her death. She had been born under the sign of Aquarius and the first label pinned on such by an astrologer is "Nonconformist." In this case there could be no argument.

Her body was anointed with aromatic oils, laid out in white satin cerements, and decked with jewelry. Her arms were crossed decorously across the now cold bosom, and, very appropriately, in each hand was placed a fine pearl-handled revolver.

It was an Indian burial and presumably the weapons were intended for use in the next world.

The grave was in front of the house at Younger's Bend. Pearl had an expensive monument erected by Joseph Daily, a stonecutter. It was of native stone and was elaborately carved. The top decoration represented "Venus," Belle's favorite horse, with the "B S" brand. On one side was a handbell complete with clapper and on the other side was a star. And in order to enligten anyone who might not grasp this rebus, it was spelled out in the stone below:

BELLE STARR
Born in Carthage, Mo. Feb. 6, 1848
Died—Feb. 3, 1889
So read the identification, and the epitaph was a poem cut out in the stone:

"Shed not the bitter tear
Nor give the heart to vain regret
Tis but the casket that lies here
The gem that filled it sparkles yet"

The poem was in quotation marks, author not credited, and the stone artisan signed his work with a J.Da" in the lower right area. It is not known whether the Belle Starr rebus of handbell and star were the idea of "J.Da" or of Pearl.

The Dallas News of March 20, 1890, carried a story to the effect that vandals had violated Belle's tomb and had stolen the jewelry along with a fine pistol which had once belonged to Cole Younger.

Some years before, this same newspaper had revealed that Belle was writing her autobiography, and it was a foregone conclusion that it would appear in that newspaper and it alone. But it never did, and it is rather certain that Belle never got around to finishing it.

In 1933, the same newspaper, usually reliable and always interesting, miraculously located the long lost little Flossie. In return for having received her somewhat besmirched genealogy, Flossie contributed a few reminiscences of Belle and Pearl. But, since she was put out for adoption at the age of two days and never saw either of them, the recollection must have been exceedingly vague.

Pearl, the "Canadian Rose," did not remain long at Younger's Bend after her mother's death. She married a livery stable owner named Will Harrison, at Ft. Smith, Arkansas, but the marriage only lasted three months. Pearl became a prostitute and then became operator of her own establishment. In time, she developed into a woman of voluptuous charms, with a glittering display of diamonds. She dropped the surname Younger, and was known at various times as Pearl, Rose, or Rosa P. Starr, Reed, and/or other legal or assumed names.

In 1894, she gave birth to another daughter. The birth record does not give a father's name, but it was reportedly rumored that he was " a prominent Ft. Smith society man."

In 1896, Pearl married a whorehouse piano player named "Count" Arthur Erbach, a newly arrived German immigrant, who played classical music. But he played out within a year. Pearl bought a family plot in Oak Cemetery at Little Rock, and buried Erbach there. She erected an eight foot monument. A few months later, their son, Arthur E. Erbach, Jr. was also buried.

The Count is commemorated with "GONE BUT NOT FORGOTTEN," and the child by "BUDDED ON EARTH TO BLOOM IN HEAVEN."

A third daughter, Jennette, by a common-law husband, was born in 1902.

On July 6, 1925, Pearl died in Douglas, Arizona, where she had registered at the Savey Hotel as Mrs. Rosa Reed.

As for Belle's son, Ed Reed, he does not seem to have played a very important part in her activities. His own life was eventful but short, and may be disposed of in one sentence. At eighteen he was sentenced to seven years in the Federal Penitentiary; later paroled, he served two more short terms for bootlegging in the Indian Territory, and at twenty-two, was killed in a shooting scrape at Wagoner, Oklahoma.

In more or less comfortable retrospect from a time now when crime is too commonplace for any glamor, we can see Belle Starr as an absurd, lawless, shrewd, dangerous woman who continues to hold her place in American folklore. The late Governor Marland of Oklahoma helped to sponsor a bronze statue of Belle, and the commission went to a well-known sculptor, Joe Morrow, whose concept seems to have been more of a modern young woman in sports costume than a frontier bandit queen. But artistic license extends far. The statue stands at Ponca City, and Belle is also memorialized at the museum in Bartlesville.

Soon after her sudden, mysterious death, the warden of the prison where Cole Younger was held allowed a reporter to interview him. The prisoner was not very communicative, but he did say that he had never been married. When asked about Belle Starr, he said with cautious gallantry, "I knew the lady slightly some years ago."

Later in 1903 when he wrote a book "The Story of Cole Younger—By Himself," he made no mention of her and their daughter Pearl.

The final frustration that Belle did not live to see was Pearl's inability to be a lady and her descent into the upper crust of Fort Smith's red light district where her house, the "Pea Green Palace," sported an heraldic device of a big illuminated red star surmounted by a glistening pearl. Perhaps there might have been a degree of consolation in the fact that Pearl had some semblance of being a lady in owning a palace, a coat of arms, and the title from staff and clientele of "Madam."

BIBLIOGRAPHY

The private lives and whereabouts of most desperadoes and outlaws were shrouded in secrecy and mystery; their freedom and lives depended on it. They were usually on the "Wanted—Dead or Alive" lists of numerous police authorities, and were eagerly sought by enemy rivals or bounty hunters as well.

A great many books and articles about these five Black Sheep have been written and published, but it is apparent that most of the seekers for truth became lost on the bypaths of hearsay and imagination. On the whole, newspapers and reputable magazines afford the most reliable and credible information, but there are other sources and we have ranged far and wide over a period of years to find them. These included public documents, police and sheriff's files, records and exhibits, private files, letters, souvenirs and memoranda, old photographs, written interviews, and visits to the various relevant locations.

It has required much patience to piece together and reconcile the conflicting evidence. Unfortunately, many interesting contributions offered by kind friends could not be used because they were not susceptible to verification. And now, considering the time involved in producing the stories of these energetic and reprehensible characters, we wonder if they were worth the trouble. They caused enough of it in their lifetimes.

Ft. Worth Star-Telegram
Dallas News
Galveston News
El Paso Daily Herald
Texas Almanac 1933, et sequit.
Colliers 1935
North American Review 1893
Texas Folklore 1924

Album of Gunfighters—Ross, Hunter
Autobiography of Americans—Van Doren
A Dynasty of Western Outlaws—Wellman
American Bandits—Gish
Calamity Jane and the Lady Wildcats—Aikman
The Daring Exploits of Jesse James—Mitchell
Jesse James was My Neighbor—Croy
Triggernometry—Cunnungham
Geography of Denton County—Cowling
Western Badmen—Waters
Life of Jesse James—Breihan
Hands Up—Waters-MacDonald
Some Western Gunfighters—Bartholemew
Sam Bass—Gard
Sam Bass—Martin
The True Story of Sam Bass—anon.
Life and Adventures of Sam Bass—anon.
Sam Bass, the Train Robber—Castleman
They Died with Their Boots On—Ripley
Belle Starr, The Bandit Queen, etc.—Rascoe
Belle Starr—Shackleford
Belle Starr and her Pearl—Hicks
Wildcats in Petticoats—Booker
The Five Civilized Tribes—Foreman
Clyde Barrow and Bonnie Parker—Cowan, Parker
Cole Younger—by Himself
John Wesley Hardin—Nordyke
Autobiography of John Wesley Hardin
Hell on the Border—Foreman

Amon Carter Foundation Files
Hedrick Collection
Witte Memorial Museum Collection
Ft. Worth Police Dept. files
Tarrant County Sheriff's files

John Selman, Texas Gunfighter—Metz
The Hanging Judge—Harrington
The Court of the Damned—Emery

APPENDIX

BLACK SHEEP WERE SEEN HERE:

ALABAMA
Mobile

ARKANSAS
Alma
Ft. Smith
Magnolia
Siloam Springs
Van Buren

CALIFORNIA

FLORIDA
Cedar Keys
Gainesville
Pensacola

IOWA
Denison
Dexter
Fort Dodge
Perry

INDIANA

KANSAS
Abilene
Bartlett
Chetopa
Dodge City
Fort Scott
Pittsburg

LOUISIANA
Arcadia
Coushatta
Gibsland
Lake Charles
New Orleans
Ruston
Sulphur

MICHIGAN

MINNESOTA
Okabena

MISSISSIPPI
Rosedale

MISSOURI
Carthage
Joplin
Mexico
Platte City
Rich Hill
Springfield
Shirley

NEBRASKA
Big Springs
Ogallala

NEW MEXICO
Carlsbad

OHIO
Middletown

OKLAHOMA
Catoosa
Atoka
Claremore
Commerce

Eufaula
Miami
Oklahoma City
Stillwater
Tulsa
Wagoner

SOUTH DAKOTA
Deadwood

TENNESSEE
Memphis

TEXAS
Allen
Austin

Belton
Breckenridge
Caddo
Cleburne
Dallas
Denison
Denton
Eagle Ford
Fort Worth
Georgetown
Grand Prairie
Grandview
Hillsboro
Houston
Huntsville
Hutchins

Kaufman
Mesquite
Palo Pinto
Rockwall
Round Rock
Rowena
San Antonio
San Marcos
Sherman
Terrell
Trinidad
Waco
Weatherford
Wellington
Wharton
Wichita Falls

978
TC

Presented by

The Tribune Chief

HARDEMAN COUNTY LIBRARY
QUANAH, TEXAS